The Pursuing and Pinoneering Culture

'Allamah Muhammad Taqi Ja'fari

Translated by
Mansoor Limba

Thoroughly Revised and Edited by
Beytollah Naderlew

Top Ten Award
International Network Inc.

2023

Published by: Top Ten Award International Network Inc.

Vancouver, BC **CANADA**
Email: Info@TopTenAward.Net
www.toptenaward.net

Ordering Information:
Quantity sales. Special discounts are available on quantity purchases by universities, schools, corporations, associations, and others. For details, contact the "Sales Department" at the above mentioned email address.

The Pursuing and Pioneering Culture, 'Allamah Muhammad Taqi Ja'fari, 1st Edition.
ISBN: 978-1-990451-95-9   Paperback

In the Name of Allah,
the All-beneficent, the All-merciful

Contents

Foreword

From the various meanings of "culture", included in this book, it seems that all societies in turn attach importance to the subject. But...

But from the author's point of view, this significant concept covers another implication that can be both studied and understood. He opens an alternative perspective to scrutinize culture after examining its various meanings detailed in encyclopedias and dictionaries, and so he detaches the content of culture from a specific individual or society, and uses this valuable term in two complementary concepts. The two concepts are: "leading culture and follower culture", which are with man from birth to the end of his life.

In the distinct view of Allameh Mohammad Taqi Jafari on human being, it could be said: Considering culture as an attribute of human being, and a human being composed of two poles (intrinsic and extrinsic), it should be noted that in order to explore attributes of human beings, all aspects of man (material as well as spiritual) should be examined, for if not taken seriously, we will definitely have an incomplete definition and conclusion. But he is still disappointed by the games played on culture and the character and future of man, considering his presentation of such a comprehensive and compassionate plan to human societies. He has concerns, objecting to the rhetoric used about high definition of "culture". Jafari firmly brings down the whip of warning in this work as well as in his other works, and like other intellectuals sympathetic to the past and present of mankind, he emphasizes the harmful results, of playing with words and names, to the human society, while he quotes Jalal-al-din Mohammad Maulvi (Rumi) who says:

The road is smooth, and under it are pitfalls,
Amidst the names there is a dearth of meaning;
Words and names are like pitfalls,
The sweet (flattering) word is the sand for (the sand that sucks up) the water of our life.

He mentions his sympathies and concerns not in order to propose an ideal prototype, but for a project that can be implemented in societies. But alas and thousands of alas... that most human societies lack caring administrators with divine and sincere intentions to implement such plans not in one society only, but in all of them.

The author constantly warns, in this work, about lack of culture as well as deculturalization. He believes that if the administrations of the societies do not heed and take thoughtful actions, mankind will turn into "machine" and culture into "anti-culture", and the history of man and humanity and even the earth will end by the selfish and the profiteers.

Allameh Jafari's institute

Culture and Its Vital Role in Human Intelligible Life

An Introduction to the Definition of Culture

Culture has been defined in a great many different ways by cultural experts and scholars. The Encyclopedia Britannica has so far[1] cited 164 alternative definitions of culture. By studying these definitions carefully, it may be concluded that some of them intend to identify certain cultural elements, e.g. scientific culture, artistic culture, literary culture, and moral culture, all of which serve only to describe various aspects of a cultural phenomenon like different artistic forms and their factors. Some definitions explain the follower culture, and some others depict pioneer culture; although they are not directly dealing with these two terms.

Let us consider a simple example to elaborate on the fact that all the existing definitions fail to form a thorough explanation of culture. Suppose a number of people are trying to find the center of a circle by spotting many points in it. Clearly, none of these points would prove to be the real center; by the same token, cultural scholars and sociologists have not taken into serious consideration the true identity of man, which lies in the borderline between nature and the supernatural:

"Truly, it was you who brought the two ends of the existence together and made them whole."

(Sheikh Mahmoud Shabestari)

Instead, they have merely studied some of the effects of the cultural elements, especially physical phenomena and cultural activities. It is needless to say that the number of physical effects could lead to countless definitions, much higher than 164. To demonstrate this, you can notice the poor attention or

---

1- Up to 1952.

neglect toward the subjective pole of culture, like the subjective pole of beauty. While culture is a bipolar phenomenon comprised of subjective and objective poles. The most comprehensive definition that can be offered in view of the existing numerous definitions is as follows:

"Culture consists of the necessary or relevant quality or way for those phenomena and activities of human material and spiritual life that are documented to sound reasoning and sublimated emotions in the evolutionary intelligible lifestyle."[1]

The elements and examples that have been discussed in the contemporary encyclopedias and dictionaries refer to both qualities of necessity and relevance. In other words, those cases and examples that are discussed consist of relevant facts and also necessities for human life. French Encyclopedia states that:

"Culture embodies the totality of knowledge acquired by man or society, e.g. a set of activities that are based on various socio-historical rules, or structures caused by changes in behavior or deeds due to specific educational conditions."

The sentences above include both, the absolute vital and also the unnecessary but relevant conditions of life.

However, as we will see in coming discussions, the necessities and relevant conditions do not totally exclude man's personal needs. Some experts believe that culture consists not of the essentials of life, like natural sciences or humanities, but of only the suitable aspects worthy of forming the basis of a culture. Here we must keep in mind two important principles:

One: The more distance between culture and natural life and fatalistic facts, and also the more evolutionary virtual facts it includes, the more human it will be.

Two: The highly elevated spiritual value according to which man constantly wishes to fill every aspect and action of his life with excellent virtues.

On the basis of these two rules, some idealistic and pioneering anthropologists believe that culture has always played a major role in the evolutionary progress of mankind.

Culture and Civilization

---

[1]-Of course, the above definition only applies to pioneer culture, whereas the follower culture does not focus on progress or evolution.

Since we declare evolutionary quality as a vital element of the definition of culture "as it ought to be", then we can use this definition regarding the civilization "as it ought to be" too. Of course, there are numerous issues regarding these two human phenomena the full address of which require an independent work. Before turning to the discussions of the definition of culture, we need shortly discuss the vital importance of genuine and perfecting culture in the intelligible life.

Concern about the Future of Evolutionary Culture

If a day comes when humans begin to lose the desire to reach harmony in dignified freedom, unconscious fatalism will put them in a mechanical life ignorant of the truth, and call it human unity. If someday the plague of deculturization infiltrates humans so strongly that it even ruins the common virtues of evolutionary cultures in various nations, it would unquestionably reveal the shameful incompetence of their leaders. Despite centuries of evolutionary endeavor by holy prophets, men of wisdom, moralists, and the sacrifices of those martyred for the sake of freedom and human dignity, social leaders today have not only proved themselves unable of uniting mankind in search of spiritual and behavioral harmony based on evolutionary cultural virtues, but have also lowered man to ignorant components of a machine. They have deprived man of the glorious life he deserves, and restricted him to only the physical desires of life, such as greed for power, dominance and selfishness. On that terrible day, which might not be so distant, history's sensitive conscience and God, who provided men with conscience to guide them through time, will take revenge on those who have demolished human dignity and values.

All authentic human cultures, holy prophets, distinguished anthropologists, moralists and those who have contributed to the culture of man's history clearly show that the only way to establish harmony and dignity among mankind is definitely through elevated virtues and morals, not mechanical characteristics and qualities. The reason is that the more man deviates from highly moral virtues, the more influenced he will be by his natural animal self. Animals also possess this kind of self –although in a more limited form – whereas in humans it handles the essence of man, for human capacities are so many and mighty that they mutually infect the universe and their peers.

The natural self knows no sympathy, emotions or logic. It totally ignores conscience, evolution and culture. However, unless these great human virtues are achieved, human unity and brotherhood would be merely a dream, for selfishness and greed for personal desires are a natural part of the animal self, which has led to the countless wars and atrocities in the history of man.

Islamic culture has thus shown great concern for the future of modern societies. Yet, some Western scholars have not only foreseen the demise of Western culture, but also believe it to be happening at the moment. Albert Schweitzer is one of those thinkers who has referred to the critical state Western culture and argued:

"It is obvious to everyone that we are heading for cultural self-destruction. What is left for us today is by no means safe, for it has not come under destructive pressure yet, and is surely too frail to be able to resist it. Modern man has much less capacity for culture nowadays, because his environment has damagingly degraded his spirit."[1]

Schweitzer believes that industrialized man is devoid of freedom, unable to focus his thoughts, incomplete, and in danger of losing his human self. He further adds:

"Society has developed so sophisticatedly that it can secretly control men, and has made him so dependent on his society that he gives up his entire aspect of thinking and reasoning…therefore, we have entered a new era of medieval times. Thought has deliberately been abandoned in the name of freedom, and men are controlled by their societies. We have inevitably lost faith in the truth, because we have sacrificed our mental independence. We have disturbed our own mental-emotional balance. Inadvertent attention in any aspect can lead to thoughtless establishment."[2]

Schweitzer considers "inadvertent struggles" another characteristic of industrial societies. During the last few

---

1- *To Have or To Be?*, by Erich Fromm.
2-Ibid.

centuries, men have been working like machines, not human beings. The essence of humanity has been contaminated, and never generations lack the necessary factors for human evolution.

"Adults are drowned in work, increasingly submitting to superficial disturbance... absolute passiveness; ignoring their own "ego" and deviation has become their physical need."[1]

In his conclusion, Schweitzer emphasizes that man should reduce the pressure of his worldly struggles and avoid frills.

Schweitzer, a Protestant, agreed with the Dominican reverand Eckhart that:

"Man should not submit himself to the spiritual isolation considered 'selfishness; he should actively contribute to developing his society to the highest possible level of morals. If nowadays only few people still possess human emotions, it is because they tend to sacrifice their piety and moral values for their own native land – they never exchange cultural values with other societies that could guide them toward high spiritual development."[2]

Schweitzer then concludes that the current social and cultural foundations are leading us to a disaster that precedes a second Renaissance even greater than the original – unless we wish to destroy ourselves.

"During the second Renaissance, mentally originated activities will prove crucial; in fact, mental activities have been the only logical and practical principal man has come up with in his historical evolution ... I have no doubt that if we act thoughtfully, the revolution will take place."[3]

However the second revolution may be, its basis will definitely to moderate selfishness, greed for power and pleasure, for without religious influence, the revolution would be impossible. It is quite likely that it be a religious revolution, which Islam – especially the Shiites – have been a waiting, in order to form a divine global society.

It is a certain fact voiced by scholars of the humanities and positive philosophies: "in our era, crucial changes are on the horizon." Whatever kind of evolution if may be, it will certainly

---

1 -Ibid.
2 -Ibid.
3 -Ibid.

concern human beings. In assessment of the coming dramatic evolution, two major theories have arisen:

The First Theory: pessimistically believes that human beings are gradually heading for spiritual and moral breakdown. Even if humans are not totally demolished, they will become selfish, greedy living beings lacking logic and conscience, drowning in their desires, and have no choice but to fit in the machine like nuts and bolts.

The Second Theory: an optimistic one, states, "The evolution will once again revive original values by considering man's intrinsic capacities for evolution, and thus regain him his true self".

Evidence shows the latter to be preferable, provided cooperation – and if necessary, even sacrifice on behalf of the leaders of the society alongside men of true wisdom and authentic scholars of culture and humanities. But if, Heaven forbid, the selfish and power-greedy keep on injuring humanity, and neglect the suicidal fall that awaits all of us, the underlying evolution will definitely follow the first, pessimistic theory – if, of course, it does not lead to the annihilation of the world and its dwellers. According to that theory, humans will be degraded as worthless as gears in a machine.

Considering man's intrinsic need for seeking excellent values and his long-established passion for evolutionary culture, and having in mind God's unquestionably wise will, we support the second theory, and predict a prosperous and encouraging future after man undergoes a great deal of suffering. Among the primary reasons for our logical optimism is the fact that man possesses the virtual desire for excellent evolutionary culture, and is always eager to protect himself from various events that threaten humankind.

The Importance of Research on Definitions of Culture

In this section, after examining comprehensive definitions of culture in various peoples and nationalities, we will come to the undeniable conclusion that since humankind essentially desires culture, he will prevail amidst all forces, greed and sensuality. As the glorious Koran says:

"God sends down out of heaven water, and the wadis flow each in its measure, and the torrent carries a swelling scum; and out of that over which they kindle fire, being desirous of ornament or ware, out of that rises a scum like it. So God strikes both the true and the false. As for the scum, it vanishes as jetsam, and profits men abiding in the earth. Even so God strikes his examples."[1]

"Generations have passed away, and this is a new generation: the moon is the same moon, the water is not the same water..

The justice is the same justice, and the learning is the same learning too; but those generations and peoples have been changed (supplanted by others).,

Generations on generations have gone, O sire, but these Ideas (Divine attributes) are permanent and everlasting..

The water in this channel has been changed many times: the reflexion of the moon and of the stars remains unaltered.

Therefore its foundation is not in the running water; nay, but in the regions of the breadth (wide expanse) of Heaven." (Rumi, Masnavi, Book VI: 3175-3179).

The Necessity of Research on Definitions of Culture

The main reason for studying the supplied definitions of culture in the best-known encyclopedias and some lexical and sociological references is to prove whether all societies of mankind believe that the true meaning of *culture* includes the proper, deserving human evolution or not, and that even if the selfish, greedy or nihilists attempt to degrade it to a paradise of banal phenomena which they call culture, it would still be false and antihuman.

Preliminaries of Reasearch on Definitions of Culture

1- It is the variety in scholars' points of view in interpreting culture that has brought about a myriad of definitions, whereas they are all in agreement about the main core of culture. In 1952 two scholars of humanities called A. L. Krober and Clyde Kluckhon in a work entitled *A Critical Review of Defenitions and*

---

1 -*The Koran*, Mc Milan, 1991; (13):17.

Concepts reviewed 164 definitions of culture.[1] As we will see later on, some of the current differences are due to time and some popular phenomena, and some others are caused by environmental features and various perceptions of ideologies. For example, *farhang*, the equivalent in Farsi for *culture*, means to pull[2]; it also refers to a branch bent down and covered with soil to help it grow, and able to be planted elsewhere.

2- The Arabic equivalent for culture, *al-thiqafa*, means triumph, intelligence and skill, and also means talent for science, crafts and life nature.[3]

3- In French, *culture* has derived from the Latin word *cultura*, which means cultivating the earth for agriculture; in also means planting.[4]

Cultura has derived itself in fifteenth century from *Colera* in the sense of fertilizing and caring. The latter word in the form of *Cultiver* was used in twelfth century in the sense of planting and fertilizing.[5]

4- In the German language, it conveys raising bacteria and other living matter on a background of prepared food; cultivating and protecting farms; and also a new group of organic living matter.[6]

And finally, in Russian it means determining the extent of man's influence on nature and his achievements in doing so.

Interrelations among Definitions of Culture

Taking the various concepts of culture throughout history into consideration, we can form a comprehensive definition: a general concept conveying victory, cunning and understanding in Arabic; planting and farming in Persian; and cultivating the soil and agriculture in Latin. However, our studies do not intend to prove that culture shares the same etymology in all lexicons and encyclopedias around the world. But we are sure

---

[1] Britanica Encyclopedia, Culture.
2 -The Dehkhoda Persian Encyclopedic Dictionary.
3 -The Jahangiri Dictionary.
4 -Larrouse Dictionary.
Dictionnaire Etymologique: de Jean Mathieu Rosay, 1992[5]
6 -Duden Dictionary.

that culture and its synonyms in the lexicons of nations of ancient civilizations, as *Duden Woerterbuch* indicates, all generally convey planting, capability of agriculture and organic life heading toward all features of fine intelligent and artistic life.

In Search of the Comprehensive Valuable Truth called Culture

Let us presume the term conveying fine valuable culture in different ethnic groups and nations throughout history – that undergoes virtual changes and has recently found entirely new meanings – is *culture*, which in ancient Persian means laying down a branch in order to raise it as a shrub, and has gradually changed to convey wisdom, education, and great intelligence. Let us also presume that the word "*culture*" has been used in its filthiest ways. However, changes in a word's meaning cannot demolish the concrete truth in *logical life*. For example, consider the Persian word "*qanoon*", which means a musical instrument. Years later it was used to convey the truth, or an important lifetime spent interpreting the truth. If we suppose that in some societies, tyrants use such words as they desire regardless of the true meanings they have, should we come to the conclusion that *qanoon* has lost its fixed meaning which refers to the relationship between man and his own self, God, the universe, or his fellow men? It would definitely be wrong, for the events depicting the relationship between man, God and other beings are unquestionably unchangeable, even if they are not termed *qanoon*.

In the next chapters, we will strive to find the fixed comprehensive truth which, whatever called, never loses its crucial role to man – unless man gives up his identity in his world of machines to such an extent that his life, soul and true self are totally demolished; or as Tyler has said, "evolve into an intelligent ape [1]", and eventually become a part in the machinery.

1-Edward Burnett Tylor (1882-1917), distinguished English anthropologist.

Chapter One

Definitions of Culture in Contemporary Dictionaries and Encyclopedias

Our research on the definitions of culture is based on the world renowned dictionaries and encyclopedias. It is obviously impossible to compile and study all of the current definitions of culture in one single volume. However, we can refer to distinguished dictionaries and encyclopedias and explore the main ones given by established scholars around the world.

Now we turn to discuss each single definition. It has to be noted that the order of discussion is based on on our access date to these sources and there is no other persuasion around.

Culture in Persian Reference Books[1]

"Farhang (derived from farhandge), [the Farsi equivalent for culture] refers to knowledge, intelligence, wisdom, accountability, a Persian lexicon, Keikavus' mother, and a branch put in soil to be planted elsewhere. It also means a water drain."[2]

Hossein ibn Fakhriddin Hassan Anjui Shirazi believes *"farhang to have six various meanings:*

First, knowledge:

"Your value has greatly elevated the heavens, and intelligence has gained much culture from your ideas."

(Kamal Ismail)

There is a valuable work by Professor Sediq entitled A History of Iranain Culture. This work contain an authentic bulk of research on the subject but unfortunately it has not said anything of the truth of culture.[1]

1- *Borhan-e-Qate* (The Undefiable Proof), by Mohammad Hossein Khalaf Tabrizi,

Second, manner.

"If man acquires culture alongside his art, will be able to manage any severity."

(Sanai)

Third, intelligence.

"One who raises war at peace-time, knows no knowledge or culture." (Nezami)

Fourth, a book containing Persian words and their meanings.

"Fate has written his name in its own desire on the pages of culture." (Souzani)

Fifth, it is Keikavus' mother's name.

Six, a branch buried in soil so that it would become a shrub and be planted somewhere else."[1]

Explaining the entry "farhang" in his Persian encyclopedia, the late Dehkhoda has cited many verses by distinguished literary figures in Persian in order to further illustrate the vast range and depth of culture in Persian literature.

The Persian Encyclopedia reads: "Culture shows a peoples' life style and traditions in anthropology. Its English equivalent was first used academically in the nineteenth century by Sir E.B. Tylor. The concept of culture has proved so useful that it is now also used in other fields of sociology, literature and biology. Culture has been the distinctive point between mankind and animals ever since the rising of man.

The traditions, ideas and conditions of a group is passed on through its generations mostly by education, not genetically. Following customs is enforced in each culture through its own special system of rewarding and punishment. Language and other symbolic tools do play an important role in the transfer of culture between generations, but some kinds of behavior can be achieved solely by experience. Every society possesses its own specific "cultural basics" which include all organizations necessary to man, e.g. social organizations, religion, political organizations, economic organizations, and material culture (tools, devices, weapons, clothing, etc.). Sophisticated societies are distinguished from "primitive" ones in the complexity of

---

1- Jahangiri Dictionary.

their cultural bases. However, these two terms must always be considered relatively.

Basically, each human community has a definite culture, but in complex societies, secondary cultures can also branch out of its national, social and religious conditions. On the other hand, peaceful or even hostile cultural contact can lead to common cultures acceptable by various nations – based on the fact that co-culturalism can exist and each side may adopt the other's traditions. The characteristics of a culture may be spread directly or indirectly among its groups. Such a process is called diffusion.

A cultural area is a land where some features of a culture are visible. Various schools of thought have emerged in anthropology attempting to account for how cultures work, develop and spread, but all agree on a vast evolutionary process throughout the history of man, especially in technical and economic domains. However, the evolution has not taken place at the same rate for all nations, and is still incomplete in many of them, although at times co-culturism can integrate several steps into one.

In the first phase, food-hunting, small groups of nomadic hunters, fishermen and fruit pickers move from one place to another in search of food. They live temporarily in caves or other shelters, as in the lower and middle Stone Age.

The next phase is producing food, in which man has learned how to tame animals and use plants. He lives in small settlements, like the upper Stone Age.

After that, civil life began, evidence of which can be found in great ancient civilizations.

Categorizing a contemporary culture should not be done solely on the basis of its technical or industrial progress. For example, today's food-hunters, e.g. native Australians are not comparable with lower Stone Age hunters 25,000 years ago, because ancient systems of relationships and religion must have been different."[1]

We may now come to consider these points:

---

[1] - Mosahab, Gholamhossein, The Persian Encyclopedia, see culture.

1.   No dictionary or encyclopedia has provided a clear-cut, specific definition of culture. The reason is not negligence on behalf of scholars in identifying culture, but due to the great diversity in cultural elements and phenomena, which prevent a fixed comprehensive definition. Neglect in achieving a complete definition could also be due to some cultural researchers ignoring its spiritual and supernatural meanings – an ignorance which has unfortunately infected some people.

2.   "Culture has been the point of distinction between man and other animal species."[1]
If we are to take into account meritorious deeds and phenomena in our definition of culture, we would have to search for the distinctions between man and animals before the existence of culture in man's fatalistic life, for some scholars consider meritorious phenomena and deeds prior to his compulsory affairs in life, e.g. thinking about preparing a settlement, developing legal relationships among a society, social management, etc.

3.   "In all, all anthropologists approve of a step-by-step evolutionary process in the history of mankind, particularly in technical and economic areas."[2]

A few points must be considered concerning the above statement:

a.   Since freedom of will is equal to authority in the definition of evolution – particularly value evolution – the technical and economic aspect brought up by compulsory life affairs therefore cannot be included in the concept of culture, as forced efforts to provide a home cannot be thought of as culture.

b.   "The evolutionary process throughout the history of mankind has not taken place at the same rate all over the world, and some cultures have not completed it."[3]
This is an absolutely correct fact, also applicable to scientific and technological progress made by civilizations; in other words, no theory or school of

1- Ibid.
2 - Ibid.
3 - Ibid.

thought is able to prove these events advancing in a direct, orderly fashion.

Anyone aware of the development of science and civilizations admits that the factors causing their existence have not only been irregular, but totally unpredictable.

c. "Sometimes co-culturism can integrate a few of the phases in the process. In the first step, food seeking, small groups of nomadic hunters, fishermen, and fruit pickers move form one place to another in search of food."[1]

Here we can see phenomena concerning culture and its mutation – which, however, due to their fatalistic nature – cannot be included in the evolutionary concept of culture.

Culture in Arabic Reference Books

The Arabic equivalent for culture is the word *al-thiqafa, which* means "victory, intelligence and skill, and also talent   for science, crafts, and literature".[2]

"Its root, thaqaf, means skillful, clever, brilliant, and victorious."[3]

To find a definition of culture and the topics concerning it, it is best to look up *al-thiqafa* and *al-adab*.[4]

Al-Monjad thus defines *al-adab*: "An *adib* is a person familiar with literature. Its plural form is oda'ba. An *adib* is well-trained in lexical and literary subjects, and possesses great culture. *Adab* means science and knowledge as a whole or a particular field. It also means what a person or object morally deserves, e.g. how one should behave in a classroom, or as a judge, etc.[5]

In the following verses also, *adab* refers to culture, and conveys   knowledge   and   demonstration   of   fine   morals

---

1- Ibid.
2- See Lessan-ol-Arab, al-marja; also Al-Monjad, thaqaf.
3- Encyclopedia, by Farid Vadjdi, see thaqaf.
4- The current encyclopedias, eg. Farid Vadjdi's, do not mention any of the recent discussions, or fervid research done on culture.
5- Al-Monjad, see Adab.

according to appropriate principles achieved through conditions in one's lifetime.

"Acquire knowledge and culture, no matter what family you may have been raised in. Culture will make you independent of any relation.

Truly, a free man is one who can claim, "This is who I am,' not "I am so and so's son." [1]

As you see in Arabic fine morals are what is intended by the word culture and it is near to the meaning that is attached to this term in contemporary world. On the other hand, due to the expansion of research and scientific development after the dawn of Islam in Arabic world the Arab scholars have made significant research on culture.

Culture in French Reference Books

Deriving from the Latin word *cultura*, it means fertilizing (soil), production, or planting. Culture also has several figurative meanings:

1. Enhancing mental strength, e.g. mental culture.

2. One's whole acquired knowledge, for example general culture, literary culture, philosophical culture, classic culture and massed culture[2] , which spread by means of mass media.

3. A series of activities based on various socio-historical guidelines, and also structures pertaining to a specific behavior or performance caused by the education of a particular social group; for instance, a special culture in the society that relates that to Western culture.

4. Culture in French has also been referred to the physique; for example, in ancient texts, *culture physique* means physical education and culturism refers to gymnastics.[3]

Another reference book reads, "In the fifteenth century, *culture* derived from the Latin word *cultura*, which means fertilizing; likewise, *cultiver*, meaning planting and cultivating was used in the twelfth century."[4]

The Rober Encyclopedia has thus defined culture:

1- It has been said that Imam Ali (A.S.) wrote these Arabic verses.
1- Culture de masse.
2- *Dictionnaire Encyclopédique Noms Communs*, Hachette, 1991.
3- Jean Mathieu, *Dictionnaire Etymologique*, Rosay, Paris, 1992.

"All of the knowledge that provides mankind with the power to criticize and the taste for judgment".

It then asks the reader to refer to words such as knowledge, education, training, and science, adding that:

"Culture is what remains in man's mind when all else is forgotten. Adjectives like vast, strong and high have been used to describe it."

Two points should be considered about the definition of culture in French reference books:

1. A careful study of the above definitions shows that the majority of the meanings provided are based on virtual facts which remain unchanged even if the objects or persons applicable to them do, unless the whole nature of mankind undergoes complete metamorphosis and becomes a helpless thing like animals or objects or parts of machinery. However, literary and philosophical culture will be unaffected, for their bases are truly unchangeable.

It is impossible to change the truly original facts shown to the French by Victor Hugo in *Les Miserables*. Even Sartre and his like, with all their novel phrases and terms tending to influence the simple-minded, failed to eliminate Victor Hugo's *Les Miserables* from the culture of mankind. Likewise, the dogmatic writers of our own era could not eliminate the role of Mowlavi's *Mathnavi* in great human culture; all they achieved was brainwashing the simple-minded with their contradicting jargon.

They felt that they were fulfilling their own selfishness, which was a grave mistake itself; selfishness is an insatiable flame that only quenches when it has burned itself out, no matter how many others it also victimizes in the process.

2. Categorizing the meaning of culture into the real and the figurative leads to three possibilities: first, some meanings may be archaic, e.g. agriculture and cultivation of the soil, which is the Latin meaning for culture. Some other meanings are frequently used regardless of their older ones. The second possibility is that culture initially meant agriculture, but through gradual use in texts of high moral values, was transformed to a new meaning. Third, the old meaning of culture, i.e. cultivating and using a potential, is an unchangeably comprehensive reality applicable to various things, e.g. the soil, trees, animals, and human beings.

Therefore, metaphor interpretations in this case cannot have a definite, evidential reason. We also must keep in mind that if a word changes in meaning, its original meaning, conveying definite true fact(s) is not necessarily omitted.[1]

Culture in View of German Reference Books

The Duden Dictionary thus defines culture:

- All of the aspects of mental or artistic life;
- the fine aspect of life;
- raising bacteria and other living matter on a platform made of food;
- cultivating agricultural soil;
- A new species of organic life.

Another reference, defining culture as all aspects of a nation's lifestyle, lists them as:

a. Human activities in order to fulfill man – and his society's – basic requirements, such as food, clothing, shelter, health care and environmental protection.

b. Providing the means needed for all human activities such as science, industry, construction, organizations, etc.

c. Efforts have been made ever since humankind inhabited the earth and culture arose with them towards providing human character with originality, finesse, and form, limiting inferior human desires and transforming them into highly elevated needs.

The first significant point about the above definition is that such encyclopedias, having mentioned the highest facts of value defining culture – such as giving form, originality and delicacy to man's character and transforming his mediocre desires into high moral needs – state that "culture began when mankind arose on earth." In other words, the facts described as meaning(s) of culture are unchangeable, and cannot be contaminated by the new worthless meanings added to culture

---

Mr. Mohsen Khalijee has helped me by translating this [1] part's French materials.

nowadays, considering "what man's talents show" and "what his values represent".[1]

Culture in the Encyclopedia Americana

"Culture, a vast concept, has been used by sociological and anthropological experts. Its other meanings refer to educated persons, i.e. those who are well-composed and are familiar with culture and the fine arts of life.

Specialized discussions on culture arose in anthropological texts of the mid-nineteenth century. Sir Edward Burnett Tyler, the English anthropologist, used the term "culture" to represent a developed series of ideas and what arises out of historical experiences. In 1910, American anthropologists used culture to show the specific characteristics of peoples in societies. In the 1930s, Ruth Benedict described culture as those patterns of thought and action that makes one distinct among others.

The word "culture" is of much significance to sociological experts, for it provides the simplest concept for expressing the behavior and history of humankind. For instance, compared to the term "society" – which, by definition, refers to an organized group dependent upon each other who coexist inside a system in order to continue their production and life – culture has vaster applications. Culture shows the behavioral content of the society. The point here is: Why has culture found so many various definitions? The reason is that culture does not consist of a single, homogeneous topic or refer to an individual. It covers many elements, including ideas, emotions, values, ends, behaviors, tendencies, and experiences."

The Evolution of Culture

Studying the process of evolution in the history of culture, we come to three significant points:
first, culture can form the distinction between human characteristics and animal norms.

Mr. Morteza Rohbani has helped me by translating the [1] German materials of this part.

Secondly, the observed behavioral pattern is due to the outcomes of man's cause–and–effect physical development. Thirdly, population growth and the cultivation of man's surroundings has led to cultural manners focusing on symbols and language, in turn resulting in a vast treasure of thoughts and ideas throughout history. Considering it through a vaster point of view, we may realize that culture is not the fulfillment of one of man's needs, but a manner-based phenomenon aiming to provide magnificent virtues of life to creatures potentially possessing it.

Man, having the capability to build tools and use them for various purposes, can obviously think of different subjects, interrelate and organize his thoughts and develop a new idea. It is also possible to pass on the findings of one generation to the next through transcription and records. No other living creature has such abilities. Culture found its true identity through the development of such commitments.

Cultural variables are based upon man's creativity and talent for imagination. Human beings are able to conceive any manner of behavior or meaning of human life. However, there are limits to practical and economic life that restrict the process of developing and establishing variable forms of concepts and social life. The economic and materialistic aspects of man's life have, in various stages, become his ability to transform his natural surroundings into higher comfort and more property. Although the artistic, research and philosophical aspects of culture have also developed, we are not sure if they have done so in certain stages. All in all, absolute diversity in cultures on earth seems to be fading away. The increase in Western, industrialized lifestyles spreading around the world has influenced many unique distinctions at the cost of replacing them with industrial civil patterns.

Historians and anthropologists believe that cultural diversity must have reached its peak during the 14th and 15th centuries; i.e. before Europeans began to infiltrate into the lifestyles of other nations.

Cultural Elements

Analyzing cultures requires certain concepts. First, we can categorize cultural elements according to quantity and basic principles. However, using specific terms will lead to the same series and usages. Apart from classifying the constituents of culture, other concepts are also necessary for research and utilization of culture. Here, we are faced with two significant ideas: concepts and actions.

Each cultural element (showing ideas on behavioral patterns, or objectives) includes all interpretations or symbols of the mental reactions of those facing the element.

The usage of a cultural element is determined by its researcher, not an individual caused by the culture. Sociologists have also categorized culture into two schools of thought, which are to fulfill man's mental needs.

Cultural Manner

Pattern-based manners can also be defined in culture using a specific method; in other words, culture can be used to define the way to do certain things in society.

Therefore, "cultural subgroups" convey certain methods for some of the actions in specific parts of the society. Thus, Afro-Americans in the United States have lifestyles very different from others, although the all live in one country. Culture used in behavioral manners is mostly applied to solve problems.

There are several points to consider here:

1.   "Its [culture's] secondary concepts symbolize educated, well-cultured people." It is incorrect to call this a secondary concept, for any individual who possesses the virtual characteristics called culture can be considered a cultural person, as we would regard anyone that has the qualities and manners of civilization civilized. The concept and term "civilization" is not a sideline concept for civilized man, and so neither is culture.

2. The text, unfortunately, does not mention the time-honored originality of cultural phenomena such as science, education, moral virtues, and art.

3. "All in all, anthropologists agree on the fact that culture, unlike instinctive or hereditary patterns, consists of behavioral learning methods and ways to adopt them."

Since cultural elements and activities concern the appropriate values of man's life, we must point out that the intrinsic culture-seeking potentials in humans are virtual, and activating them calls for need and conscious effort. For example, the potential need for acquiring science, art and moral virtues exists in humans regardless of time or geographical issues, but using it in reality requires education and practical admittance.

4. A considerable point in the Encyclopedia Americana is, "The term 'culture' is of high importance to sociologists, for it provides the simplest concepts needed to express human behavior and history. For instance, compared to the term "society" – which, by definition, refers to an organized group dependant upon each other coexisting inside a system in order to continue their production in life – culture has vaster applications. Culture shows the behavioral content of the society."

It is true that culture is highly important, but we must note that its importance is not due to the fact that it provides the simplest concept expressing the history and behavior of mankind, for the simplicity of a mass abstract noun, such as law, pleasure, sorrow, generosity or reality cannot possibly lead to its comprehensive explanation. Therefore, encyclopedias and dictionaries have begun research to find the complete truth about culture – and have so far led to around 164 definitions of it – likewise, much effect has been put into research on the concept of law.[1]

This is the best reason for the complexity in the definitions of culture. The fact stated by the encyclopedia, "Why has culture found some many various definitions? The reason is that culture is a homogeneous topic and does not pertain to one individual alone; it covers a great many elements of high diversity, such as ideas, emotions, values, intentions, actions, tendencies and experiences," needs more accurate

---

1- See *Culture: A Critical Review of Concepts and Definitions*, by A.L. Kroeber and Clyde Kluckhohn, quoted in the Encyclopedia Americana.

consideration, for it is true that the various definitions of culture are not homogeneous. This best proves that finding a comprehensive commonality among the existing 164 definition has not been what all the dictionaries and encyclopedias have been struggling for. Considering the diversity among human souls, it would be extremely hard to do so, even in case of the examples we have mentioned (emotions, values, goals, actions, tendencies and experiences).

5.   The theory that "Culture shows the behavioral content of the society", depicts the resulting outcomes of culture, not the facts facing it.

In other words, the theory believes that the culture of a society lies in the behavioral aspects of its inhabitants; however, it does not mention the intrinsic factors of culture, i.e. moral virtues and aesthetic values. Considering the principle that "no effect can totally reveal its cause," our objection is quite justified. For instance, much effort is made nowadays to advertise a culture like goods all over the world. Is the reason behind these aesthetic efforts truly serving mankind, or to increase consumer demands? Those who regard culture a purely behavioral subject should have a convincing explanation ready for such problems.

6.   The Encyclopedia Americana states three points about the evolution of culture:

> **First:** "Culture is exclusive to humans, not all living beings." This point, as far as our knowledge of biology is concerned, seems to be totally accurate.
>
> **Second:** "Such behavior is a result of cause and effect outcomes in human physical development."
>
> This point calls for a more scientific analysis; if "human physical development" means that a significant extent of cultural effects appear as intrinsic outcomes in the body and its development (such as mental, emotional, etc effects), it is quite reasonable; however, if this means limiting cultural effects in the physique, it would not be acceptable, since human spiritual evolution by means of internal factors such as religion, accountability, morals, love and humanitarianism proves highly more fruitful than depicting physically human cultural development.

Thirdly: the fact that "Population growth and the consumption of natural resources, have caused cultural norms to result in a treasure of ideas and approaches throughout history, based on symbols and language," can also be accepted, except a short point of interpretation that is necessary about "cultural norms." Since there is no comprehensive definition of culture in such texts, "cultural norms" remain unexplained.

7.   The text reads, "Considering the vastness of culture, it is not what primitive men invented owing to their needs; culture is a manner-based phenomenon tending to supply beings with the great moral life they potentially had."

This theory calls for more careful attention, for mutual coexistence between men and the serious cooperation and harmony it demanded, was undoubtedly essential; in other words, the gradual necessity of force balance and sacrificing endless personal desires – which caused destructive disturbance – led man to accepting limited desires in order to make mutual coexistence feasible. This was the beginning of coexistential culture, which was established by men in completely free will, not by force. The text then states, "Man, who is able to build tools, and use them in different jobs, can definitely also think of various ideas, interrelate them, and come up with new ones." Obviously, as the need for physical tools existed, human spiritual life also needed the most basic cultural factors.

Let us consider the following statements in order to further elaborate on our point:

"Delicate philosophical ideas and elevated religious beliefs are generally intertwined in legends, like an ore containing both coal and gold. Unless mythological analyses separate myth from ideological units, it would be impossible to explore the treasures of human thought buried in legends.

Regardless of the entertaining lullaby-like aspect of myths and legends, in fact, it is the existence of such highly original thought supplies unconsciously lying in various contexts that makes studying mythology inevitable for researchers of the history of the development of philosophical schools of thought, anthropologists, sociologists, theologists, idealists, scholars of humanities and literature, and those who aim for awaking the conscience of mankind.

One of the best ways to discover the basic origins of legends is definitely compiling an alphabetical glossary of the main terms and concepts, and comparing them with other common national or foreign legends."[1]

Distinguished historians also agree on this:

"It is not logical that arts and supernatural facts such as man's desire for beauty, truth, the good – generally, the "ideal" – are totally separate from the physical needs he fulfills in order to stay alive. The reason is that we believe the best way to a successful life is to feel that human life is a meritorious truth.

Some experts have come to believe that primitive men struggling with their surroundings, either found no chance to discover their spiritual truth, or felt no desire for the *internal* tendencies towards eternal facts and supernatural discoveries. However, scholars who know human nature correctly, believe that primitive men were not obsessed with the practical aspects of life like their predecessors are nowadays, and even had spiritual affairs, and used their emotions to color the objects around him, to look beyond their natural appearance and realize their supernatural meanings. Thus, the emotional values lying in objects became more significant than their natural features. If we consider carefully the life of ancient Australians in the vast plains – usually thought of as the poorest of people due to high violence and social maladjustment – we would discover from the mysteries in their lifestyle, that even every cane or stone they used contained historical or traditional characteristics. Therefore, canes and stones used in ancient eras, were related to secrets in the human surroundings of that time that are not conceivable now. However, man did consider himself the happiest creature on earth.

In brief, since the earliest times, men have been both physical and spiritual; both realistic and idealistically perfectionist." [2]

1- Africa, Legends of Creation, by Uli Bayer.
2- History of the World, Hamerton, Vol.1.

8. The text says, "...culture is a part of human creativity and imagination as a manner of life – the basis for cultural variables. Man can conceive almost any behavioral state or interpretation of human life. There are, of course, some obstacles on the way to establish stable forms of social and life variables, due to biological and economic realities. The economic and materialistic aspects of human life have apparently in the course of time turned into the transform of his natural environment into greater wealth and luxury. Aspects of culture such as arts, research, and philosophy have developed in some periods, but their continuity is doubted. All in all, cultures of the world are losing their absolute diversity. As modern industrial lifestyles spread throughout the world, many rare cultural diversities have been sacrificed to make way for industrial civil life. Anthropologists and historians believe cultural variety to have been at its peak during the 14th and 15th centuries – shortly before European began to infiltrate the lifestyles of other countries."

There some points in the above statements that require further study and criticism:

a. The statement, "Cultural variables are based on creativity and imagination" is generally correct and acceptable, but the point is that the cultural constants inside humans need to be discovered and distinguished from variable cultural examples; the above statement not only ignores this point, but even makes it more mysterious later on in the passage: "All in all, the cultures on earth are apparently losing their diversity."

b. The text reads, "Man can conceive almost any behavioral state or interpretation of human life."

The above sentence is somewhat ambiguous, for if the physical outcomes of human behavior are meant, they are obviously noticeable through studying ideas and senses by means of behavioral research. And if the focus is upon the total identity and internal and external results and reasons for human behavior – as most scholars around the world have admitted, the number of human faculties and capabilities that still remain unknown far exceed his known abilities; such a general statement would require revision. This is also applicable to the next phrase- "interpretation of human life, "for our knowledge of the true nature and factors of the existence of living beings is extremely meager, so our interpretation of life would be highly limited and superficial. Let us consider the theory proposed by a distinguished Russian biologist:

"Every object in the world can be thought of as both living and lifeless. Accepting such an approach makes such questions like "What is life? What objects can be considered alive, and which cannot? How did life arise?" meaningless. As we know, the definition of "life" is still struggling in dispute, and many scholars have failed to achieve it."[1]

After comprehensive research on life and its development, he adds:

"It is only by means of such an evolutionary approach that we can not only discover what goes on in the bodies of living beings, but also provide answers to the seven million "whys" we confront on our path to discovering the true essence of life."[2]

However, since discovering why the phenomenon "life" has progressed so evolutionarily is as hard as the other discoveries about life, we must say that discovering the true essence of life in every object, makes us face seven million "whys" plus one.

c. It then comes to the conclusion that:

"However, the diversity among cultures on earth is apparently fading away. With industrial Western lifestyles spreading out throughout the world, some rare diversities have disappeared to make way for industrial civil life."

The encyclopedia unfortunately refuses to mention any of the causes or positive/negative outcomes of its predictions.

We must first address the problem whether cultural diversity on earth is deteriorating by itself, or by fate, or powerful dictators striving to strip man of any freedom, dignity or the life he deserves?

We then face the question whether industrial societies spreading throughout the world will destroy only the rare

---

1- Life, Nature and the origins of Evolution, Oparin .
2- Ibid.

differences or influence all cultural distinctions and therefore also abolish the identity of culture itself ?

The first statement, "The diversity of cultures on earth will gradually fade away", implies that an identity named culture will not be able to withstand Western industrial lifestyles, which is likelier than other possibilities. If so, there would be no creature called "man" on earth any longer, and no sign of his great potentials, abilities, ideals and beauty either. In other words, if Western industry dominates the world, we would face a clockwork of machinery instead of man or humanity. If such a vision embraces reality, and man loses his life, culture, ideologies and ideals, the motive for living would either remain or be destroyed; if the latter proves true, the world would turn into a huge industrial factory, which may continue functioning until its resources run out, but will eventually destruct; that is, of course, if the greedy dictators allow life to last so long.

On the other hand, if the motive for life survives, it will overflow time and time again, bring industry under man's control and prevent life from being sacrificed by ignorant dictators and anti-moralist gluttons for power. In other words, when culture vanishes from the earth – the background for the evolution of man's life – it would definitely mean the end of life.

9. The encyclopedia does not go into explaining definitions, classifications, significance, changes or transfer in "cultural elements", so we cannot make any comments on this matter.

10. The encyclopedia presents a definition of culture in order to elaborate cultural styles, but does not explain the nature or fundamentals of culture. If what the author(s) have tried to convey is merely that "culture can by applied to certain social procedures", their concept of culture is not at all clear.

After our study and criticism of the treatise on culture presented in the encyclopedia, we may undoubtedly claim that since the main issue here is mankind, it is impossible to achieve any acceptably true facts about the highest of human concepts – such as culture, just to name one – which all nations, even the most industrially sophisticated, may agree upon unless we all come to an agreement on the identity and characteristics of man.

Culture Seen by the International Grolier Encyclopedia

"In biology, culture refers to a group of living cells or organisms grown artificially, such as several kinds of microorganisms like bacteria, yeast, and fungus growing and reproducing in a medium. The word 'culture' has two main applications:

1. It refers to any product of a great civilization, such as art, literature, or philosophy; therefore, it could colloquially refer to highly educated persons.

2. Anthropologists use the term 'culture' to distinguish man's history and life. For instance, the creation of ideas, thoughts, habits, and objects leading to man's ever-complicating coexistence with his surroundings.

In this book, we shall deal with the second meaning of culture, which has academic and historical usages. The latter meaning of culture leads to three major domains:

a. culture as an evolutionary concept,
b. culture as a descriptive concept,
c. culture as a lifestyle or human behavior.

The development of the concept of culture also depends on the above categorization. At first evolutional research (such as Darwin's studies on biological evolution) appears. Then we come to descriptive treatises on culture, coinciding with the early 20th century developments in research on peoples and cultures. Finally, various cultural forms and changes in human behavior are to be studied.

As an evolutionary concept, culture indicates those characteristics that distinguish man from other animals; characteristics that have evolved through million of years since life arose on earth. The fossils found from the Ice Age made by humans or humanlike creatures, each provide a history. Wherever there is a sign of thought or conscious human activity in order to control or respond to his surroundings, there is also culture.

Such evidence, in the shape of stone tools at least 700,000 years old, alongside Autralopithecus fossils has been found in south Africa."[1]

Culture in the World Book Encyclopedia

"Culture is a term that sociologists apply to all patterns of life. Colloquially, culture means activities like arts, literature, or music, but sociologists also include in it all thoughts, imaginations and all methods made by a group. Therefore, arts, beliefs, habits, innovations, inventions, language, technology, and traditions are all part of culture.

Civilization is a term similar to culture, except that civilization pertains to highly sophisticated patterns of life, whereas culture is a way of life; whether simple or consisting of detailed ideas, culture is made up of ways man has learned to behave, feel, or think (and not his involuntary biological functions).

Any human being works, understands, and thinks in a manner that shows his culture. In other words, culture refers to functions man as learned to work, understand others, or express his ideas more efficiently.

Some animals, guided by their genetic instincts, follow certain patterns of behavior. Animals naturally inherit the methods of searching for such requirements as food or shelter. The distinctive point between man and animals in this case is that man is capable of experiencing alternative methods for providing his shelter, and achieve better results through his own attempts. There is no end to man's struggle towards faster, easier and better achievements. Culture consists of a series of experiences acquired by every part of the human body.

Sigmund Freud, the well-known Austrian psychologist, sees culture as an artificial instrument man uses in order to improve his physical faculties (like dentures or glasses). He believes culture, like any other man-made tool, enables him to do what his body could not manage. For instance, if man had

1 - International Grolier Encyclopedia (Mr. Ali Lotfi has helped me by translating the materials of this part).

arrows, he would not require forks or hooks; if he had tame horses, he would never have to run; and without culture, he would not be able to send astronauts to the moon and provide them with enough technology to survive.

The human body needs oxygen, a certain temperature, and many other necessities in order to remain alive. Likewise, man-made instruments and other cultural facilities enable him to overcome the limitations of his unpleasant surroundings and survive."

Then the text goes on to define primitive culture as a simple survival tool, and quotes Sir Edward Burnett Tylor's definition of culture:

"Tylor, the distinguished English anthropologist, defines culture as other scholars do nowadays. In his 1971 book on primitive culture, he defines culture as:

"A series of any beliefs or ideas (general or complicated) including science, ideologies, arts, morals, law, traditions and any other habit or capability man may have acquired as a member of his society."

The origin of human culture dates back to prehistoric times. Some milestones in its process can be named as:

1. The development of tools and instruments,
2. The rise of agriculture,
3. The growth of large cities,
4. The progress in scribing and calligraphy."[1]

The article continues with explanations on each of them.

The World Book Encyclopedia presents five different viewpoints in defining culture:

1. Culture as all modes of life (Sociologists).
2. Culture meaning various activities, e.g. arts, literature, and music.
3. Folk culture includes all thoughts, mental perceptions, and methods for performing group actions. Therefore, culture consists of arts, beliefs, ideologies, traditions, inventions, innovations, languages, habits, and technology.
4. Culture consists of the modes man acquires in his behavior, emotions, and thought (except his involuntarily biological functions).

1- World Book Encyclopedia (Mr. Mohammad Baqer Jalali has translated the materials of this part).

5. Culture includes all experiences gained by various parts of the body.

The text finally introduces Frued, who considers culture equivalent to the most normal of tools and absolutely natural phenomena limited to the physical aspects of man's life. The most significant definition given in the text pertains to Tyler.

Surprisingly, the fourth definition contradicts the fifth; the fourth definition separates man's "naturally biological" functions from culture, whereas the fifth – particularly Freud – says nothing about supernatural phenomena or facts.

How Does Culture Change?

All cultures are constantly changing. Changes may happen rapidly or slowly. Since culture consists of various factors, changes in one will also affect the others. Some sociologists believe many social maladjustments are due to unequal changes in different cultural components. When some parts tend to lag behind others, cultural retardation develops.

Most of the cultural retardation observed in the history of the United States concerns ideas, traditions and mental matters. Science and technology advances so rapidly that it often overtakes culture and leaves it behind. Therefore, guiding the leaders of technology today – who lucratively provide themselves with power and authority – toward more consideration for human culture and moral virtues may prove in vain, or perhaps cause them to become even more resistant toward it, and strengthen the advance of technology.[1]

Therefore, it is best to address societies where the fundamentals of human culture still exist, and hope for a day when they lead a cultural renaissance.

A point ought to be emphasized here, although we will address the issue when we explore disharmony in cultural elements. The point is that unfortunately, scholars currently presenting definitions and characteristics for culture, do not

---

Saeb Tabrizi rephrases this maxim in the following words: [1]
Don't cry by the oppressor as we have seen
Kebab's tears cause the fire get infurated

distinguish the stable sections of culture from its variable parts. The unchangeable cultural elements depending on man's fixed needs should be distinguished from the change-prone elements; however, the two are usually integrated, which leads to errors in cultural activities and understanding. Let us now consider the general, unchangeable principles of culture, which are not to be mistakenly mixed with its variable examples. For example:

1.   Eagerly seeking perfection is an undefiable principle, despite the variety of its outcomes in different people.

2.   Respect, which is reflected in human cultures in forms such as love and devotion for fellow beings.

3.   Man's intense need for a meritorious life.

4.   Adjusting and correcting the quadruple relationships: man-himself, man-God, man-universe, man-fellow beings.

Culture Seen by Argentine References

"Culture ethymologically means cultivating the earth and reflects the relationship between men and the earth, although its meaning has undergone change through time. The simplest definition of culture describes it as a series of physical and spiritual advantages a human community acquires in order to establish harmonious coexistence in its national society."

Argentina's scholars, lexicographers, historians, philosophers and even revolutionary anti-imperialist sociologists have defined culture as mentioned above. As well as being a true fact existing outside man's physique, culture also has mental aspects. Most intellectuals have failed to understand the comprehensive quality of culture, for they are obsessed with individualistic civil culture (and also affected by Imperialistic culture infiltration), and therefore cannot realize how vast the concept of culture really is. It goes far beyond that, in fact. This is why we are addressing Chinese, Spanish, French, and Latin American cultures.

Imperialism is constantly influencing the masses, "democratizing" cultures by imposing its own imperialistic culture, luring intellectuals towards its anti-revolutionary goals, spreading huge amounts of publications and movies. By presenting imaginary tales of big city life and imperialistic center lifestyles, they create a mirage of a luxurious life. They have thus bestranged millions of their own culture by spreading American patterns of life. Although America has presented the lifestyle, Americans themselves are devoid of historical or cultural background. In South America, native cultures were unable to resist imperialistic propaganda, so alien cultures succeeded in separating the middle and well-to-do classes from the country's national culture. As imperialism falls astray now, native and alien cultures, still in constant conflict, continue to divide the people. The first impact reflects in arts. It is not surprising that is South American folk art (in Brazil and Mexico, for instance) shows significantly political background. The reason is the endless folk culture and increasing revolutionary conscience of third-world South American artists."[1]

We now should point out a few things concerning the above text:

1.	The briefest definition given here for culture is the same as the comprehensive one presented in other well-known encyclopedias. Since we have already treated them, there is no need for further elaboration.

2.	"As well as being a true fact existing outside man's physique, culture also has mental aspects." This is absolutely correct, and we will address it later on in our discussion entitled: "Culture is a Bi-polar Truth."[2]

3.	"Culture is also a historical reality." Considering the definition of culture and its historical effects, it is obviously a reality arisen from man's original needs.

4.	"Intellectuals are mostly unable to understand the comprehensive identity of culture." The reason is the great diversity among cultural elements and outcomes, which inhibit a comprehensively common concept. However, if we consider culture as a progressive reality, we may present a definition based on the one given during the first sections of this book, which can include all of the elements and outcomes of culture:

1- *The National Identity of Argentina*, by Juán Jose.
2- P. 142.

"Culture consists of the appropriate qualities or meritorious methods for man's spiritual and physical activities, based on logical thinking and emotions arisen from sensible evolution."

5.   The other reason mentioned why the comprehensive identity of culture has not been understood, lies in cultural invasion – and also due to Imperialistic cultural invasion." We have already mentioned that the issue currently is not cultural invasion, but deculturization, for in order to generalize and globalize culture according to the definition above, obviously invasion and opposition are totally unnecessary, for all of mankind eagerly desires a culture so developed that it would guarantee their spiritual and physical evolution.

6.   "By influencing the masses, 'democratizing' culture and imposing Imperialistic cultures, Imperialism is luring intellectuals towards its own anti- revolutionary goals."

"Democratizing culture" is equivalent to "follower culture", which totally neglects the moral, political, literary, artistic or religious development of man, for the motto of follower culture can be defined as:

"What I want is certified, only because I want it."

7.   "By mass-producing publications and films, they are constantly deteriorating the minds of the masses. A mirage of a luxurious life is created through showing fairy tales of big city life in Imperialist centers. Millions have been infatuated by American lifestyle propaganda, and have become estranged with their own culture."

Such statements need no further comment. However, those who lead the operations aimed to destroy other cultures should have in mind that all human societies resemble a swimming pool, if in which a small stone is thrown in its corner, waves large and small will diffuse in all parts of the pool. The adverse results of destructing cultures will definitely infect all human communities. Once, a father got angry with his young son and said, "I will take you by the ear and swing you around the yard". When his son asked, "If you do so, father, will you swing, too?" The father immediately let go of him. He was a highly intelligent father, for he at least valued his own safety.

8.   "Millions have been alienated from their culture."

This magnificent statement reflects its writer's deep thoughtfulness and sense. It is clear that pioneer cultures affect human souls so profoundly that their destruction will lead to the deterioration of man's own identity.

9. "Foreign and native cultures still divide people into separate groups, which are constantly in conflict."

Cultural conflicts can damage every aspect of people's social lives.

Culture in the Encyclopedia Britannica

"Culture can be defined through man's behavioral characteristics, as well as other factors affecting his behavioral development, especially culture, language, ideologies, habits, traditions, laws, social organizations, devices, techniques, works of art, religious rituals, ceremonies, etc. The existence and the application of culture strangely depends on a particular human faculty, which is commonly called the capacity for sensible or abstract thought. However, since strong evidence of sensible thought has also been reported in animals, the meaning of "abstract" falls into doubt. Therefore, we had better express man's unique capability to abstract through the term "symboling". Symboling includes selecting symbols to represent specific objects or events unable to be realized through our senses.[1]

A good example is verbal eloquence. The sound included in the word "dog" provides no hint of its meaning. Obviously, its meaning arises from a conventional agreement selected by humans. Symbol selection is a behavior independent of the physical senses.

Alternative Definitions of Culture

As Edward Burnett Tylor, the English anthropologist stated in 1871:

Symbolling should not be confused with symbolizing. [1]
These two words have different connotations.

'Culture consists of a complete series of knowledge, beliefs, arts, morals, laws, traditions and any other abilities, capacities or habits acquired by man as a constituent of his society.'

According to Tylor's definition, culture is attainable only by humans. His statements won the approval of other anthropologists for fifty years. Advances in anthropology, however, led to deeper studies on identity and concepts, and in turn various definitions.

In 1952, two American anthropologists, A.L. Kroeber and Clyde Kluckhohn cited 164 different definitions of culture in their work, *Culture: A Critical Review of Concepts and Definitions.*

In their view – and also as many other scholars nowadays see it – the best definition of culture consists of an abstraction; to be more precise, abstract human behavior.

Such concepts prove to be either incomplete or vague. The existence of behavioral patterns – frameworks of behavior, whether inherited genetically or acquired socially – have been undoubtedly proven in nonhuman species [e.g. honeybees, ants and termites].

The abstract concept of culture poses first the question whether culture is real (for abstraction is at times considered inconceivable); secondly, it defies the existence of culture. Therefore, as the non-biological science of humankind, culture cannot exist without real visible phenomena, for it has been regarded as both real and nonexistent.

Kroeber and Kluckhohn eventually concluded that if culture were regarded as equivalent to behavior, its identity would bring it into the domain of psychology. Therefore, their conclusion was that culture consists of abstractions of observable behaviors.

Now rises the question how we would abstract wedding rituals or pottery according to Kroeber and Kluckhohn's pattern? Such questions lead to problems they have not considered. Perhaps Leslie A. White's solution in his 1959 work, *The Concept of Culture,* may prove useful. White argues that, "The point is not whether culture is indeed a reality or a mental concept; its scientific interpretation should anyhow be carefully studied. Anything or any event leads to behavior when studied in relation to human organisms. When studied not in relation to human organisms but to others, it becomes culture – for instance, the prohibition against marrying one's mother-in-law or stepmother consists of a series of concepts, attitudes, and actions. If they are regarded in relation to human organisms, i.e. the organism's functions, they can be named behavior. Therefore, if we consider the prohibition against marrying one's mother-in-law or stepmother in relation to social compositions, settlements, traditional segregations of man and woman and their roles in society and upholding the good, it could be regarded as culture.

This distinction has been used for years; many words are considered behavior due to their pertaining actions. However, if words are considered in relation to each other – studying their lexical definitions, grammatical and structural usage – they will become part of language, and would enter not only psychology, but also linguistics. Thus, culture is a term referring to a category of items and events depending upon conventional symbols studied in a framework of the supernatural content of man's life."

Now let us consider the points of importance presented in the Encyclopedia Britannica:[1]

1. "Culture can be defined through man's behavioral characteristics, as well as other factors affecting his behavioral development, especially culture, language, ideologies, habits, traditions, laws, social organizations, devices, techniques, works of art, religious rituals, ceremonies, etc."

The problem with the above statements is that:

a. Including culture in its own definition does not seem to make sense, for the defining items ought to be clearer than those, which are to be defined; using an object to elaborate itself traps us in a vicious circle.

b. Including particular human behavioral patterns in the definition of culture is not sufficient, for such patterns, e.g. language, belief, and habits, express only a few of the results of culture, not culture itself: "The existence

---

Dr. Abdulrahim Gavahi has translated these materials for [1] me.

and application of culture calls for a uniquely specific human faculty".

Obviously, unless that unique faculty is known, the true identity of culture would remain unsolved, particularly since the results of cultural elements are so diverse that sometimes it is impossible to combine them into one general concept that can be called the identity of culture. For instance, works of art that oppose morals or religion cannot be united to convey culture. The encyclopedia thus elaborates on the cultural faculty:

"Such a faculty is commonly known as the capacity of logical or abstract thought."

It then objects to this term, and adds, "However, there is proven evidence of logical thought in animals, so the meaning of abstraction here is unclear."

We must say that even if living organisms other than man possess the faculty of logical thought, they would be incomparable to man, for human thoughts are conscious, and definitely use abstract principles. In nonhuman life, as far as we know, it merely moves from the beginning steps to results; in other words, their actions aim for providing the beginning steps, like nesting as a preliminary step towards mating and reproduction.

However, the statement, "The meaning of abstraction is unclear" reflects an obvious mistake about the delicate functions of the brain. Some people think that the functions performed by the brain and everything pertaining to the "self" can be studied by the same methods used for physical phenomena. They ignore the fact that we will never be able to discover the true identity of self-consciousness. However, a developed brain is not only self-conscious, but also capable of understanding and performing abstraction. Describing such internal functions is as hard as explaining joy, sorrow, surprise, or responsibility.

c. "Thus, symboling is a more suitable term for expressing the unique capacity for abstraction in men."

We must remember that symboling, as other words, is just a conventional term, and cannot reflect its content. Two illustrating examples can elaborate this point in the subsequent sentence.

2. Culture is "a complete set of knowledge, beliefs, arts, morals, laws, traditions and any other capacities or habits acquired by man as a member of the society".

If the above-mentioned phenomena refer to interrelated realities affecting each other's qualities and also quantity, their combination can express the unique reality named culture; however, we have already seen that deriving a definition of culture is not possible merely through determining one or several culture phenomena.

The statement, "If we could maintain a relationship with the whole identity of culture through identifying cultural phenomena, we would no longer need to fully comprehend the definition of culture" is incorrect, for it is based on the false premises that we can establish a relationship with the whole identity of culture by identifying a few cultural phenomena; the ability to figure out the true identity of objects merely by studying a few of its effects is a grave mistake. In proof of it, we must say:

Primordial Origin of Human Eagerness for Understanding the Truth of Life-giving Culture

It is proven clear to any researcher on culture who has accomplished discoveries about it that without culture, man would not only lose his dignity, self-respect, his valuable "freedom" and the life he merits, but even consider them as harmful hallucinations; as we all know, if such basics of life vanish, the only logic remaining in man's individual or social life would be the passageways to nihilism, power and pleasure. Obviously, if power and pleasure dominate man's life, no necessity or meritorious value could prevail, and even their opposing factors would also be demolished, even though they may be justified.

More surprisingly, most academic authorities on the – humanities still continue to attempt to prove the fact that man is heading for true greatness, with such deceiving eloquence that any simple mind believes them. Some put on such a detailed display of complex jargon that even other scholars might be forced to assume it to be unquestionably true. High claim for man's progressive evolution aims to sacrifice all of the cultures and peoples around the world – who basically agree on logical principles – to feed their technological monster. One day, the monster might strangle its own operators to death, and eliminate any chance for them to relive their painfully eventful story, which ends in suicide.

A significant point comes to attention here, which can also influence human life evolution: all around the world there are hundreds of seminars, conferences, and vast studies on man and his relationship with technology, and still, there is no indication of a serious attempt to discover an intelligible identity of culture and its relation to humankind. Perhaps the few honest authorities on humanities are totally in despair about the unstoppable demise of humanity.

Therefore, let us uphold our heartwarmingly reviving culture and introduce it to other people, and have community leaders do their best to help the process – before it is too late. Then, they will definitely admit that ruling over one human being who enjoys dignity, logical freedom and the life he/she deserves, is better than ruling over millions devoid of them, who have only been labeled "human" by history after the Cromagnons.

3. "As Kroeber and Kluckhohn and also many other currently leading scholars see it, the best definition of culture consists of an abstraction – to be more precise, an abstraction of human behavior." If the above sentences refer to a dimension of reality, not only is it generally correct, but in fact Kroeber and Kluckhohn have pointed out an important aspect of culture (the internally innate pole) which is also the abstract aspect of culture. This is an absolutely correct point, for the non-instinctive, calculated movements and accountable behaviors observed in some animals, refers to meritorious values conveying the general concept of culture, which is undoubtedly abstract (as is the general concept of beauty). The regular behavior seen in honeybees, ants and termites depends on their unconscious instincts, not conscious merits or freedom; therefore, if Kroeber and Kluckhohn believe the abstract definition of culture to be the best one, they are gravely mistaken. It would be like defining beauty as "an abstract concept", which reveals nothing at all about the qualities or identity of beauty.

In brief, we must note that the general truths about culture – beauty, greatness, etc – consist of two poles: the first, the primordial pole, which includes mentally abstract concepts describing general definitions. The other pole is observable, i.e. those behaviors and effects seen physically.

Thus, we may put the theory of culture being an abstract concept in the encyclopedia in opposition with Kroeber and Kluckhohns's viewpoints. The encyclopedia states that:
The concept of culture as an abstraction poses first the question whether culture is real (for at times, abstraction is considered inconceivable), and then defies it."

The authors of the encyclopedia must keep in mind that defying abstract realities such as culture, beauty, and greatness could first cast doubt upon all scientific principles – which are definitely derived from generally abstract issues and regular phenomena in the world – and then even question the integrity of mathematical and geometrical laws. Such a presumption could put all of human knowledge and everything man has acquired through mental abstraction in the shadow of serious uncertainty, or even defy them all.

4.   The encyclopedia states that, "Therefore, as the non-biological study of mankind, culture would be consistent both nonexistent and real, and could not remain without actual worldly events."

Unless interpreted correctly, the statements above could prove unreasonable, for if we judge the reality of objects biologically, we would have to defy all of man's psychological activities, for they are non-biological.

It is scientifically reasonable to accept the existence of internal, psychological, and mental facts, even though their external effects would require observable behavior and imagination in visible phenomena.

5. The statement, "Therefore, Kroeber and Kluckhohn concluded that culture is an abstraction of observable behavior" flaws in its sense-based deduction is that Kroeber and Kluckhohn have neglected the distinction between the facts that "Observable behavior provides the basis for abstract mental realities like culture, beauty and justice" and "Observable behavior leads to the abstraction of culture".

Scientific observations and analyses on abstract facts have shown that culture, beauty, justice, etc, are bipolar abstract facts (consisting of subjective and objective poles), and the resulting behavior account for the observable one. It is incorrect to suppose that such realities arise from abstractions of observable behavior.

6. We may conclude from the above item that Kroeber and Kluckhohn's conditional theory – "If culture is regarded as identical to behavior, it would naturally become a psychological issue" – calls for some rethinking, for bipolarity should not make culture a domain of psychology, as is the case in beauty consisting of two pokes (internal virtues and external virtues).

However, such issues can be studied in terms of psychological and also scientific matters, but they do not necessarily afflict their abstract reality.

7. The text reads, "Perhaps Leslie A. White's suggestions presented in his 1959 work, *The Concept of Culture*, may provide a solution. White reasons that it is important to take into consideration the scientific interpretation of culture, not whether it is a reality or just a mental concept."

This point also needs to be modified, for in order to fully comprehend the scientific interpretation of culture, it is at least as important as other essential factors defining culture to determine whether culture is a really external fact or just mental – if not the most important, for the qualities of a mental fact highly differ from those of physically observable ones, even if the two share a common abstract concept. It then adds:

"Whenever objects or events are considered in terms of their relation with human organisms, they lead to behavior. Otherwise, i.e. when they are considered only in relation to each other, they would by definition result in culture."

The point rising here is, what is meant by "objects and events" in relation to human organisms? If they mean all – external or internal – factors and motives, the point would prove to be true, for human organisms are obviously prone to any external or internal influence, which lead to behavior, whether being merely a reflex or causing mental or bodily functions. However, if "events and objects" convey externally physical phenomena, they would only account for a certain extent of behavioral factors.

On he other hand, the statement, "If studied independent of human organisms – i.e., only in relation to each other – they would by definition result in culture," is somewhat unclear, for billions of the components of the universe are constantly affecting each other, but many of such effects may not fit into culture. As we have already seen, the primary basis of culture is the virtually internal pole relating to human life merits such as "What it is like" and "What it *should* be like", which lead to man's aims and ideas in such issues.

8.　"Thus, culture is a term referring to a class of objects or events depending on conventional symbols considered as part of man's supernatural content."

Culture as Seen by Russian Encyclopedias

According to the encyclopedia published in 1946 the culture is defined as follows: "Culture is a series of social achievements consisting of physical or mental advances used by the community, and also those cultural traditions serving man's future progress.

In societies suffering from struggling classes, culture inevitably becomes class-biased. The opposite of culture is barbarity, savagery, or culturelessness. A true understanding of culture is only feasible on the basis of socioeconomic guidelines and sequences of social organizations brought about by defining productive forces, productional processes, social relationships and the qualities of any given society.

Yet, culture cannot replace these concepts, for it includes all achievements of any range – mental or physical – altogether, whose characteristics determine historical periods for various societies, peoples, or nations.

Culture consists of man's creative activities, and is the most significant sign of his advance level. Culture derives from the Latin word *cultura* (agriculture), which means mowing, producing and processing; it originally conveyed man's influence on nature, determining his achievements and the factors playing a role in them. The latter meaning was most used in the bourgeois culture era, and was seen frequently in the works of 19th century historians, anthropologists and archeologists, which led at that time to the term "The History of Culture".

The concept of culture consists of two parts, physical and mental. The physical aspect shows man's ability against the forces of nature. Physical culture conveys man's progress in understanding nature, the community, and also the scope of his vision and progressive thoughts and knowledge. Tools are the most prominent symbol of physical culture.

Mental culture consists of social achievements in morals, arts, science, and philosophy. It also represents man's political and legal relationships and advances. Mental culture is used to determine the extent of progress made in social, political, or legal relationships. Language, speech, thought, logic, and behavioral principles make up the phenomena of human life." [1]

The following comments may be presented on the above statements:

1. It is true that culture is of high importance in man's progress, and as a principle, the main role of culture is to be progressive.

However, what eventually can be named pioneer culture? The question is left unanswered.

2. The statement, "In societies suffering from class struggles, culture inevitably becomes class-biased" is correct from a certain viewpoint, but on the other hand also calls for reconsideration. What is meant here by "struggling" classes? If the struggle involves positive competition instead of harmful conflicts, culture can definitely serve the development of such a

---

1- Constantinov, *Encyclopedia of Philosophy*.

progressive society. Also, if we were to have a systematically organized community, culture would again prove to be dynamically progressive, and aim for the advancement of the whole society.

3. "The opposite of culture can be stated as barbarity, savagery, or culturelessness."

The important point seen here is how meritorious culture is, despite those who regard it as social customs and traditions. No matter how deserving and elevating social traditions may be, we based the definition of the identity of culture (given at the beginning of this discussion) upon its meritoriousness. Therefore, since the highest human virtues and principles make up culture – and defying them would defy the whole of humanity – "The opposite of culture is barbarity, savagery, or culturelessness."

4. Further on, we encounter two contradicting statements:

a. "A true understanding of culture is only feasible on the basis of socioeconomic guidelines and sequences of social organizations brought about by defining productive forces, productional processes, social relationships and the qualities of any given society."

b. "Yet, culture cannot replace such concepts, for it includes all achievements of any range – mental or physical – altogether", for understanding a true fact means acquiring knowledge of it without the influence of any presumed principles or accepted ideals.

In other words, it is scientifically vital to strongly avoid using our physical senses (laboratory devices, tools enhancing human senses, etc) as much as possible to discover realities as they truly are. By gathering more experience and knowledge, we can free ourselves from the conflicting points in our scientific domains.

Culture in Italian Encyclopedias

The definition of culture in the Italian Encyclopedia is as follows: "Culture is the series of mental and social knowledge which can be acquired through vast study – though never completely.

A cultured person aims to develop intelligent thought in himself/herself, feel it flowing through his body, and use it to quench his mental desires. In fact, he tends to activate his peers' – or even his predecessors' – thoughts, and purify their mental processes.

The most dangerous enemy of culture is fashion, which can demolish all cultural values. Fashion tends to constantly substitute novelties for the old. It even destroys itself.

The history of culture is an average of the tastes, knowledge and moral and/or religious beliefs existing in a certain location and era.

Civilization consists of the artistic, scientific, econo- mical and moral life aspects dominant over a nation, era or all of mankind.

Culture depicts intellectual lifestyle and thought, and its reflection upon a generation or a country. This definition obviously also conveys the concept of civilization in Italian.

Culture, derived from *cultivure*, means planting, developing a farm; it also conveys all of man's mental or acquired knowledge, especially academic levels of literature, art, music, history, philosophy, etc.

Culture is not only a mental issue, but also spiritual, relating various branches of knowledge (as its spiritual aspect) to developing tastes and attitudes.

As a generalization of the above statements, we come to the culture of a nation, era, or cultural development and the history of culture.

In anthropology, as well as sociology and psychology, culture is considered a human community's organization or characteristics, including the goals, virtues, symbols, beliefs and behavioral patterns common among most of its members."[1]

Let us now take a few points helpful to our under-standing of culture into further consideration:

Translation of these phrases have been conducted under the [1] supervision of Mr. Angelo Michele Piemontese Italy's cultural attaché in Iran.

1. "Culture is the series of mental and social knowledge which can be acquired through vast study – though never completely."

Clearly, although this definitions presents some components of culture to a certain extent, the identity of culture – the main core of the definition – remains unmentioned nevertheless.

Two points are worth considering:

a. It is undeniably true that acquiring the whole of mental or social knowledge requires vastly extensive study.

b. Such vast studies would still prove inadequate for achieving complete mastery of culture and its components and outcomes.

2. "A cultured person aims to develop intelligent thought in himself, feel it flow through his body, and use it to quench his mental desires."

This statement shows man's authentic eagerness for culture. Indeed, when man selects his culture consciously and freely, he must have found it sufficiently deserving for him to feel it flow through his body and quench his intellectual needs with it. Obviously, no sensible person, consciously aware of his benefits and perils, would choose an animal or filthy quality as his culture, or become so attached to it that it would flow through his/her veins. This is the virtual meritoriousness a dynamically objective human culture should have. Otherwise, the significant species known as "homo sapiens" would definitely disappear from the face of the earth.

3. "The most dangerous enemy to man is fashion, which demolishes all cultural values."

If only today's cultural leaders would carefully and adequately consider this critical issue – the conflict between fashionism and a dynamic, objective culture they could save mankind from a hemlock that deviates man's spirit from following his virtues, pulls people so deeply into consumerism that it demolishes their health, possessions and dignity, throws their spirit into the darkness of despair and infidelity, wandering in artificial ruins made by their greedy rulers.

As the encyclopedia states, "Fashion is always substituting novelties for the old"; therefore, fashionism and dynamic, original cultures would always conflict, for if man does not use his enormous sense of novelism in order to gradually renew his spiritual and psychological virtues, he would undoubtedly apply it to superficial fashion games. Cultures of dynamic originality are based upon fixed principles much higher than changes in appearance. The encyclopedia puts it very delicately: "Fashion can even destroy itself."

4. "The history of culture is an average of the tastes, knowledge and moral and/or religious beliefs existing in a certain location and era."

Provided that the above statement is *based on the permanent principles of the culture*, it would be perfectly correct: the history of the culture of a given society at a certain point of time and location can be expressed by the average of tastes, knowledge or moral and/or religious beliefs based on permanent human principles, not the average of variable, baseless outcomes of alien cultures spreading from one society to another. If it is not stated it the basis of fixed principles, however, it would prove prone to defiance.

5. "Culture includes intellectual lifestyle and thought, and its reflection upon a generation or a country. This definition obviously also conveys the concept of civilization in Italian."

As an indication of one of the aspects of culture, this statement is correct. But further elaboration on "intellectual thought and its reflection upon a generation or a country", especially "intellectual thought", may reveal one of the most important constituents of the definition of culture.

6. "Culture is not only a mental issue, but also spiritual, relating various branches of knowledge (as its spiritual aspect) to developing tastes and attitudes. As a generalization we come to the culture of a nation, era, or cultural development and the history of culture."

These valuable statements prove that the identity of culture does not only reflect the thought of a community; likewise, the thoughts of the members of the society cannot represent their culture either. The spiritual aspect of culture, i.e. man's evolutional development towards high moral virtues, consists an important part of culture, and would be worthless without it.

Culture Seen by Greek Reference Books

"*Cultur* is of a Latin origin and means agriculture. In the last two decades, however, ideological and social class changes turned it in Greek into *cultura*, which means agriculture, and also physical and mental development through education, evolution, culture, and intellectual training.

Greek dictionaries provide agriculture, education, training, culture and civilization as its synonyms. Occasionally, when one is labeled as *culture yaris*, it humorously means a person pretending to be interested in cultural matters in order to show off before others.

In Greek, culture is seldom consisted of a series of meanings, for Greek is such a vastly rich language that there is a specific term for each object or concept; therefore, the five synonyms provided for culture are easily applicable to their proper cases, each of which convey a certain aspect of culture."[1]

He are the three most significant points arising from the definition of culture in the Greek Encyclopedia.

  a. Its cultural elements are mostly of evolutional value, and the world "development" is stated.
  b. It introduces 'intellectual training" as one of the concerned parts. Obviously, "intellectual" cannot be limited to mere thought, but must include mental activities based on moral virtues.
  c. Culture conveys variety: "In Greek, culture is seldom consisted of a series of meanings, for Greek is such a vastly rich language that there is a specific term for each object or concept."

We will discuss this significant point further later on.

Culture as Seen in Spanish Encyclopedias

The Royal Spanish Academy's Dictionary metaphorically describes culture as "the result of developing human knowledge and perfecting it through practice".

The materials of this part has been translated by Mr. Ali [1] Asghar Farshchi.

Space Calpe, the best-known Spanish encyclopedia available, defines culture as being "the mental or physical developmental state of a nation or peoples".

The encyclopedia considers illustration (*illustracon*) and civilization as synonyms for culture. *Salvat* presents a philosophical definition of culture:

"The series of definite productions of humans as creative beings able to change themselves as well as their surroundings."

The definition provided in the Royal Spanish Academy Dictionary is more likely real than metaphorical, considering its frequent usage and approval by the *Space Calpe*. Perhaps this mistake (which also occurs in the French encyclopedia) lies in the lack of distinction between a word's actual meanings at a certain time with those other points of time, which is caused by the expansion of the depth of meanings of a word as time goes on.

Considering the Latin origin of the word – meaning agriculture, fertilizing, and raising plants and living beings – the subsequent meanings of culture arisen in Eastern countries may also be associated with the original ones as its examples, results, or even real meanings – education, fertilizing human knowledge, or purifying it through practice. If there were nothing in common between its new meaning – "the mental or physical developmental state of a nation or peoples" – and 'civilization' and its old ones, even if the older meanings were contradicted, they would still remain real. In other words, culture would be a verbal portmanteau among various realities.

The second statement, "The series of definite makings of humans as creative beings able to affect themselves and their surroundings" also depicts the element of man's innovativeness and his capability to change his environment.

Culture as Seen by Chinese Encyclopedias

The *Sea of Chinese Words* thus defines culture: "All of the physical of spiritual wealth created by man throughout social history consists culture. Culture is a social phenomenon, and each society possesses a culture appropriate to its own social physical development. As an ideology, culture represents the politics and economy of the society, which greatly affect its socioeconomic survival. In class-orientated societies, culture also has class-biased qualities.[1]

Proletariat culture, critical of man's historical achievements, makes use of all the experience gained from class struggles, productional struggles, and academic experiments and develops."

The above definition brings us to several points:

1. The statement, "All of the physical and spiritual wealth created by man throughout social history makes up culture" implies that *The Sea of Words* considers all of these treasures as culture; in other words, each of these components cannot individually be culture. Unless, of course, supposing the components of the definition were not related, and the omission of any of them would not demolish culture. Therefore, it is obvious that we literally mean "all", and culture includes each and every one of its components.

2. In order to define the identity of culture by using a definition, the words forming the definition should be clearer than culture (the "defined"); yet, culture nowadays is more easily understood than words like "all of the physical and mental wealth", etc. by people.

3. How can physical wealth possibly be included in the meaning of culture?

4. "Culture is a historical phenomena." This is absolutely correct, provided that we accept that culture arises, continues and evolves throughout history, rather than being fatalistically brought about by it, for our definition of culture was based upon "qualities" and ways of a meritorious, sensible life. Therefore, since fatalistic phenomena totally ignore values and merits, culture cannot depend on fatalistic historical factors.

5. "Each society possesses a culture appropriate to its own social physical development."

The following point shows that this statement calls for revision.

The materials of this part have been translated by Mr. [1]
Muhammad Hussein Taremi.

The fact that each society has an appropriate culture of its own is not applicable to all cultural phenomena or elements, for throughout time and even today, human societies share a series of cultural commonalities like literary culture, artistic culture, moral culture and ideological culture; although each of these concepts differ characteristically in aspects such as literature, arts, morals and ideology, cultural diffusion from one of these aspects to another in one society or among several societies is quite common. If nations and peoples were not basically so common in culture, today's vast mutual cultural understanding could next exist. The phrase "social physical development" verifies our point, for if we were to evaluate a society's cultural development on the basis of its physical production growth, finding a few common points of qualitative and quantitative growth among some societies would definitely lead to common cultural elements.

6. "As an ideology, culture represents the politics and economy of the society, which greatly affect its socioeconomic survival."

In comparison to an original Chinese economic, political and legal theory – "Economic affairs, especially those concerning production and its tools, quality and quantity make up the most fundamental element of every aspect of human life, whether economy, politics, morals, law, etc. – the above statement is contradicted, for it believes that culture (an ideology) determines the socio-politics and socioeconomics, whereas the theory states that politics, economics and even culture are reflected by fundamentally important economic affairs. The current harmony in manufacturing methods and financial viewpoints and also the vast difference existing among cultures and ideologies requires more careful attention.

Due to its political viewpoints, the definition provided for culture in the Chinese encyclopedia has undergone deep reconsideration by scholars today. However, had Chinese scholars considered their vast history and culture more carefully, they would have found an incredible wealth of cultural elements rarely found in any other society. Perhaps the originality of diverse cultures in China has led to the tumultuous early to mid-20th century cultural diversities.

As *The Ancient History of Chinese Philosophy* reads:

"The general trend during this era was destructively sceptic, casting criticizing doubt upon all basic foundations, even family and marriage. Liang Chi Chao (1873-1929), the well-known scholar, compares it with the Renaissance in Europe. Indeed, all of the thoughts of this era are closely related to the sociopolitical events occurring then. Christianity has found strong support in China, bringing with it Western knowledge and philosophy, particularly John Dewey's pragmatism and Karl Marx's dynamic theories; both have had profound influence upon Chinese intellectuals. Distinguished writers like Tolstoy, Ibsen, Guy de Moupassant, Shelley, Emerson, Marx and Engels have had a strong effect on causing such a novel atmosphere." [1]

As we will see, a certain viewpoint rising in order to determine the fate of culture cannot destroy the original cultures of a civilized society.

"Philosophy develops alongside other political, social, religious and artistic changes, all of which are used to depict the culture of a country. Therefore, it would be natural for a primary school of research criticism to arise during this last phase of total changes, and put the new Confucian eras of Song and Ming up to ridicule. They are China's most meticulous critiques ever. Although their radically critical ideology can be regarded as pragmatistic, it would still not qualify as a philosophical school of thought, for it emphasizes the study of language and criticizing texts rather than truly philosophical research. Criticism, in fact, as the most effective motivation during this era, could itself lead to a new school of Chinese philosophical principles.

The consequent effect of such critical spirit is the movement entitled "New Culture." Its leaders, hailing Western positivism and pragmatism as their major inspirations, and the knowledge of social development and democracy as their goals, regarded

---

1- The ideas of such personalities would definitely differ a great deal, or even contradict. Merely supposing that they were influential in the Chinese society, sufficiently proves that China must have possessed a culture to prepare its intellectuals to accept such a vast range of diverse – or contradicting – schools of thought.

the Confucian primary school equal to their predecessors' conservatism. "Down with Confucian and his followers," was their motto. However, it was not easy to demolish the ideals of millions of Chinese people, and a struggle began – and, sadly, still goes on.

Once, all was turned inside out, except for China. Now, however, nothing in China has escaped change. The most conservative nation in history has become the most radical, and tends to demolish all traditions once regarded valuable, all organizations, monuments or moral and virtual norms. However, it is not possible to destroy ancient ideas and customs established since the era of ancient philosophers, and replace them with Marxist ideological brainwashing. The old virtues and morals still remain engraved in peoples' minds. The Chinese prefer harmony, compatibility and composition – none of which fit into Marxist ideologies. Knowing this, Communists have attempted to adapt Marxist-Leninist theories to suit traditional Chinese humanitarian beliefs.

This does not mean that Chinese philosophy is robust, for as we have already seen, it is all but that.

Although Chinese philosophy – as of other nations – has suffered much change and upset, very seldom has it adopted anything from foreign cultures without adapting it specifically to Chinese philosophy. In fact, the natural harmony within Chinese philosophy is the key factor to its flourish. Any influences not adjustable to its evolutional harmony have faded away."[1]

As Durant quotes from Hu Shih:[2]

"Taking the innovative trends of philosophy in 5th, 4th and 3rd century China into consideration adds to its respect."

We must state that Hu Shih, although a pioneer of the "New Mutiny Movement", has intelligently recognized how worthy his predecessors were, and thus expressed the most important issue in his country:

1- Chu Jai, Winberg, *Ancient History of Chinese Philosophy,* and Will Durant, *History of Civilization*, Vol.1.
2 Hu Shih (1891-1962), Chinese philosopher.

"If accepting a new civilization would mean uprooting the old rather than combining with it, mankind would undoubtedly suffer extremely heavy losses."[1]

Therefore, the real question is how we can adopt a new half-civilization able to adjust itself to our own, and survive."

Culture in the Japanese Encyclopedias

Culture has thus been defined in Japanese reference books: "Efforts towards making use of nature or natural resources in order to improve man's life.[2]

a. Knowledge, arts, religion and man's spiritual achievements.
b. Technical achievements equivalent to civilization. The word culture means:
   • civilization,
   • civilizing, and
   • Gentleness and exquisiteness."

In the above-mentioned definition of culture, both bringing into use natural talents and resources in order to improve man's life, and the highest human capabilities, talents and phenomena, e.g. science, arts, religion and other spiritual achievements have been included.

In item b, civilization has been cited as one of the meanings of culture. Civilization, growth, evolution and development and other such concepts can all be regarded as results of culture, for culture – by definition[3] – is what links all definitions; culture determines a society's goals and ideals, and indicates guidelines and motives to attain them. However, we must keep in mind that the results – civilization, development and evolution – in turn affect cultural elements.

In all, the definitions of culture in Japanese encyclopedias clearly affirm the evolutional, meritorious reality of culture.

1- Will Durant, *History of Civilization*, Vol.1.
The materials of this part have been translated by Mr. [2]
Hossein Kazempoor.
3- See P.2.

Culture as Seen in Indian Encyclopedias

The following themes define culture according to Indian perspective in general terms and after that we directly address the definition proper of culture: "As a whole, civilization in India is more alive than anywhere in the world, and one of the oldest. Few countries have been conquered, and even fewer have such diverse climate, traditions and languages as India. The reason why Indian civilization has survived is the harmoniously structured legends and social values, which have found their true identity after fifty years of struggle, gradual acceptance, and evolutional combination. In a country as vast as India, alien occupation, war or victory (the factors leading to harmony or decomposition in empires or kingdoms) have not caused India to suffer the emigration of its population, another culture replacing its own, or physical influence on its nation's customs. The key to survival in India lies in certain organized customs, beliefs and qualities its nation possesses; Dharma and keeping on with the four balanced aims in life:[1] Artha, the desired ideal, Karma (deeds), Moksa (freedom) and deliverance, all of which rule people supernaturaly.

The final word on India's civilizational achievement is that one's *caste*[2] or actions are determined by one's Dharma inductions. Every individual should search, study and eventually elevate a certain series of approved rules and duties based on the necessities of life.

In his work *Mahabharata*[3], Krisna[4] describes Dharma as a protective activity, consisting of social order and universal harmony, both of which prevail in the Indians' minds. It is such a divinely universal justice that forms the rules making and protecting the universe and logic.

Dharma has depicted and adjusted peoples' social life and attempts towards their goals, and has been described throughout history as the undisputed key to the existence of

---

1- The four elegant Buddhist realities forming the base of Buddhism.
2- Indian religious sect.
3- The great legendary Hindu book.
4- One of the three Hindu Gods described in Mahabharata.

social relationships and liberating forces arisen from mutual dependency and unity.

The individual end, attaining perfection, also the communal end in culture, is achieving undisputed balance and reality in man's universal existence and universal society (*paramataman*)– worshipped and named *Narayana* in Indian – both of which mutually depend on each other.

The Hindu Philosophy of Culture

"The most logical, powerful and glorious representation of Indian philosophy and culture is undoubtedly the statue of the heavenly spirit *Shivamahayovara* (three sculptures in one), located in a temple on the island Elephanta.

The main face of the absolute, bright sculpture – *tatpurusa saclastiva* – does not face any direction, and is located beyond its own limits.

Aghora, the figure on the right, looks fearsome, angry and aggressive, and is a symbol of disapproval and destruction. The left figure, *Uma*, Shiva's bejeweled wife, represents positive games and movements, love and affection."[1]

In Indian culture, *Uma* (also called *Secti*), carrying a water lily, is a symbol of Artha and Karma goals. Aghora, the right figure carrying a snake through his fingers, symbolizes Dharma goals; Moksa, righteousness and liberty, whereas the main figure – Tatpurusa – considers the harmonious and repetitive structure of nature, silence and activity and peace, all to be temporary. Like any other phenomenon, they rise, reproduce and then decompose.

Universal legends and forms, along with symbols, statues and the pictures seen in many sacred Indian books have played a significant role in spreading Indian culture, and even provided a framework for studying Asian cultures, and giving them form and structure.

More significant examples of these legends are: Jatakas, Puranas, Agamas, Tantras and single texts like Saddharma, Lalitavistara. Only through scholasticism, literature and art can one understand the spirit of India, the inspirations throughout its history and its relationships with the outside world. India's

---

1- Radha Kamal Mukerjee, *The Culture of India.*

fundamental cultural references, and all of its classes of people, even those descending from nomadic, Iranian, Syrian or merchant ancestors, sooner or later were dominated by the idea that life is temporary. The necessity of moral virtues (Karma), emigration, belief in the existence of spiritual social ranks, the sacred and dynamic form of family life and responsibilities, the ideal of brotherhood among men, expressing affection for others, aesthetic attitude towards life and its consequential emotions and desires, have arisen in a both abstract and centralized manner.

These social virtues – which form the generalities of a civilization – must have been supernaturally human for its basics, unity, expansion and generalization to be used frequently throughout time, helping form empires and renaissances, and keeping people's zeal for life burning in times of despair.

Geographical Influences upon Cultural Expansion

"Culture is an anthropological term including everything, from the customs people follow when they eat or produce coal to how they construct their buildings; the social, moral and religious virtues highly popular to them, or the accepted trends used to satisfy the more intellectual minds. The fact that India more or less succeeded in protecting its protected cultural evolution, is partly due to the geographical features of the country, whose location has kept it away from excessive visitors.

Furthermore, the Himalayan mountains form a natural barrier in the north of India, preventing invaders and keeping Indian culture quite safe."[1]

The most striking fact about Indian culture is:

"The individual end, attaining perfection, also the communal end in culture, is achieving undisputed balance and reality in man's universal existence and universal society (paramataman) – worshipped and named narayana in India – both of which mutually are dependent upon each other."

- Ibid 1

Considering such evolutional principles, belief in god and the supernatural, we should also take other Indian cultural elements into consideration.

Indian culture is incredibly unique among all other cultures throughout the world – whether old and new, Western or Eastern. In a nutshell, all positive or negative capabilities imaginable for man can be seen in Indian culture. It includes a variety of issues, from purely scientific approaches to man and the universe, and even absolutely mystic, philosophical and fictional approaches. As some scholars on India have claimed, "India is like a mass of coal containing lodes of diamond."

1. Here, there is a variety of beliefs, from pure idealism to realism, from the goodness of mankind to his lethal threats, and also a vast range of theories, speculations and conclusions on the universe, God, egos and so on.

2. Indian ideologies are mainly religious, and are accepted owing to peoples' religious faith. Will Durant's theory on it is quite worthy of consideration:

> "Religion is incredibly strong and important in India – more than any other country. The fact that Indians have been conquered many times by alien rulers shows that they do not care who dominates or exploits them. The main point was religion, not politics; the spirit, not the body; the immortal other world, not this mortal, worthless life.
>
> When Ashuka undertook absolute piety, he nevertheless remained faithful to the Hindu religion, which shows the powerful influence of this religion on even the strongest of men. In the present century, again it was a man of piety who united all of India for the first time throughout its history, not a politician."[1]

This proves how profoundly critical the role of Islam has been in guiding mankind and uniting religion and politics.

Religion cannot merely be regarded semantically, i.e. by only considering supernaturalities, and ignoring materialistic, economic, legal, political and artistic affairs, or issues adjusting human life virtues, for none of man's potentials cannot embrace reality without a logical connection between man's physical, social and worldly affairs with his supernaturally spiritual. It is

---

- Will Durant, *History of Civilization*, Vol. 1.1

such neglect of man's life in the four relationships (man-himself, man-God, man-universe and man-other humans) that has led to a Persian saying, "Ever since he broke up with his dear aunt, he's been thinking about conquering India." Will Durant's mistake in interpreting Ghandi's attempt to liberate India was ignoring the fact that managing all the tedious social activities of negative resistance is impossible without knowing the principles of politics, even though the negative resistance against the enemy may be a religious and spiritual one; since moral, religious, political, legal and revolutions should be based on man's original needs, any constructive revolution must have been established on the basis of human spiritual motives. Hence, some sociological experts have stated that any change truly advantageous to humanity, must definitely arise from religious motivation.

Animism in Indian Culture

Animism is quite common throughout Indian culture, although it is mostly based on emotions rather than reasonable deduction. With the exception of feeling the existence of God, its essence is the highest, most significant feeling of humans, especially because the higher the essence is, the more elegantly glorious it will be. However, there are several points of significance to be considered on this cultural element:

    a.   How valuable is well-reasoned life? Is life virtually so gloriously priceless that man can do nothing but sacredly respect it?

        This is incorrect, for any living thing of any situation, does not necessarily possess highly valuable merits; even man, the most complete of all creatures, is at times so dangerously rotten that he is ready to destroy millions of lives – maybe even the whole world – for just a few moments of his own pleasure. If man cannot justify bloodthirsty tyrants like Ghengis Khan or Neron, he would find no other reality provable either. Has God truly created such glorious value in life?

        The answer is yes, but we must keep in mind that although God has granted man the potential for glory and valor, the potential is variable; like the God-given potentials for dignity and grace, for which if man does not choose the path of righteous morality, he would be doomed to fall.

The phenomenon called life is also seen thus in a value-based point of view, i.e. life is the phenomenon which man was given the God-given potential to make real; therefore, when used unlawfully, the potential would naturally fade away, or even turn into anti-life and disturb other living things. In such cases, life will fall into anti-values.

Hence, no original human culture is able to absolutely uphold the value of life.

b. Would a culture regarding life as so extremely valuable, allow a group of people claiming to be supporters of culture to slay human beings influenced by propaganda and politics, without confirming its lawful, critical necessity for life? In other words, despite having a strong element like essentialism of life, how does Indian culture explain the killings of Muslims there?

c. The belief that meta-psychosis leads to a great deal of suffering and at times loss of life – and provides the chance for greedy tyrants to ravage their country – also needs reconsideration, for if human logic fails in such cases, the existence of "intelligible life" [1] would no longer be acceptable.

Having studied Indian culture, we now address a few concepts concerning culture in the Academy of Lalitkala:

"An academy determines national stability, as well as the perfect character, capacity and facts of life, and continues on its way despite the immense contradictions remaining.

A life which guides the compulsory forces and activities of man's natural life towards evolutionary goals by means of more freedom of choice, thus, the human character is gradually developed and guided towards the highest end of life having found the answer to six fundamental questions (Who am I? Where have I come from? Who am I with? Where am I? Why have I come here? Where will I go from here?) – contributing to the harmony of the whole universe, dependant upon divine greatness. [1]

Keeping on with such ideas about protecting cultural heritage, establishing a knowledge of the arts among people, and encouraging creativities and visual arts in a vast scale, have been some our academy's goals."[1]

These statements contradict the following, for the former describe culture as an everlasting flow, whereas the subsequent state, "Anything going on alongside with people is human culture ... human beings have unstable behavior, which varies with time and location. Human societies and behavior have constantly changed throughout history, and new findings and experiences have influenced man's behavior. Likewise, man's experiences, culture and behavior affect all social influences. Therefore, culture should be regarded as a part of our man-made surroundings."

As you see, besides contradictions in describing culture in stability or variation, considering human behavior as original is also another one of the current superficial deductions of the text. Unfortunately, such anti-cultural imitations have spread out of Skinner and Watson's[2] works into other societies. As we have frequently repeated, few parts of the humanities have escaped the destructive harm of behaviorism.

Culture in African Encyclopedias

A. Kenya

"Culture is peoples' lifestyle used in a certain period of time in order to deal with social, political and economic challenges. Kenyan culture has originated from three native communities:

1. The Cushites (the Buran, Somali and Randil tribes)
2. The Nilotes (the Luvo, Kolenjin and Masaee tribes)
3. The Bantu (the Kikoyo, Lohya, Lamba and Mijkenda tribes)

Kenyan culture in general is influenced by its tribal organizations, and is a mixture of several native tribe cultures."[3]

- *The Encyclopedia of India*.1
- Contemporary originalist theorists.2
  The Encyclopedia of Kenya.3

This definition is obviously limited to the applications of culture, not its definition or characteristics.

B. Namibia

"After Namibia declared independence, since English was accepted as the sole official language of the country, the definitions for culture in its reference books have also been derived form English encyclopedias, despite diverse cultures dominating the various ethnical groups and tribes existing in the country.

For example, each ethnical group tends to express respect for its own tribe's customs and traditions in affairs like marriage, food, manners and morality as the culture of the whole society, whereas non-native emigrants from Europe and South Africa bring along a culture totally different from the Bushmans or other primitive tribes.

In general, the definition may be stated as the capability of various tribes and communities to adapt oneself with public laws.

The English-based definition moved on to – and even accepted by – Namibia or other African societies cannot convey the essence of "true culture" in these societies, as laws transferred to other countries are unable to meet their real legal needs. Therefore, it is added, "despite diverse cultures dominating the various ethnical groups and tribes existing in the country".

If the imported culture exceeds the native in strength and executive quality, it would definitely dominate the country; however, the established ideals, beliefs, and logical conscience-based ideologies are too strong to fail to resist foreign cultures.

C. Other African Countries

By referring to expert research on African societies, we can address culture in other countries in Africa. Uli Bayer, for instance, has presented highly significant material.

"Delicate philosophical thoughts and highly religious beliefs have always existed beside simple-minded superstitions in legends; they resemble a huge ore of coal, containing randomly distributed lodes of diamond. Therefore, unless we do not extract them out of

the fairy tales through analysis of the legends and divide them into primitive thought groups, we may never be able to discover the essence hidden inside delicate human thoughts and legends.

As a matter of fact, besides the playful lullaby-like aspect of legends and fairy tales, it is the existence of the most original resources of human thought belonging to various peoples in them that make researchers of philosophical thought, development history, upholders of human conscience, anthropologists, sociologists, theologians comparing different religions, ideologists and other scholars of the humanities and folklore literature inevitably attracted to them."[1]

The significant point about culture in African countries is that, unlike other continents where political, economical, legal and cultural changes happen gradually, highly intense changes in Africa have since the earliest times defied the usual process, turning primitively virtual culture into a complicated network dominated by technology.

Clearly, African countries have suffered two kinds of cultural invasions, which can be categorized according to social and cultural lifestyles:

- The culture of the invading societies;
- Generally mechanistic culture, relatively close to their national culture.

The rise of religious cultures like Islam and Christianity in Africa has, of course, familiarized them with spiritual cultures, which aid them to live by principles common in other main cultures of the world.

Culture as Seen in Polish Reference Books

"Culture means the series of achievements made by human civilization activities throughout its evolution. Creative activity by people constantly enhances these achievements. Culture also determines the extent of progress made by the society or a certain class of people, which depends on natural forces, the level of public knowledge, artistic creativity and forms of social coexistence. The term "culture" is applied to various aspects,

---

1- Uli Bayer, *Africa, Legends of Creation.*

and finds different meanings in fields like literature, scientific texts, and everyday conversation. Many years ago, culture was categorized to:

1. Physical culture, meaning tools and equipment and also skills used in social production and enrichment.
2. Mental culture, including all scientific, artistic, social organization, and moral achievements.
3. Individual culture, conveying the culture of the individuals in the society.
4. Tool culture, conveying all physical advances.

Currently, a different type of categorization is used to define culture. On this basis, culture means:

1. How we express (language, attitudes, behaviors),
2. dominating nature (industry, techniques, and health care)
3. social organizations (the government, law, morals, ethics)
4. individual knowledge (religion, the supernatural, ideology),
5. artistic or literary creativity, and
6. mental activities (knowledge, science)."[1]

Culture in Finnish Encyclopedias

"Culture: **1.** (seldom used to convey) agriculture or planting several shrubs, **2.** (main meaning) situation of physical and spiritual accomplishments (and all of their effects) made by man, a nation or a group of people at a certain period of time, **3.** *a)* expanding physical and spiritual abilities and characteristics, *b)* exquisite beauty in customs, traditions, and the value expressed in the arts or generally in any other aspects of human life."[2]

"Culture: civilization, agriculture; primary meaning: farming.

- *The General Encyclopedia*.1
- The Finnish Dictionary.2

1. Protection and development of natural surroundings, land, plants and animals in order to fulfill man's vital needs.
2. Human activities and productions achieved in technology, science, arts and religion.
3. Man's spiritual development.
4. The essence of a nation's (or a group of nations') greatness.

Culture can be categorized into various cultural domains like customs, mental conceptions, education, lifestyles, justice, politics, science, arts and religion."[1]

The first statement – "(seldom used to convey) agriculture or planting several shrubs" is quite significant, for it requires the Latin meaning of culture (agriculture and other pertaining meanings to it) – which later infiltrated into most European dictionaries and encyclopedias – to have been the oldest one, which has been cited by the authors as a reminder alongside the newer meanings. Since the attention to the archaic quality of agriculture as a meaning of culture has been fading away in Finnish and other encyclopedias – and even in conversation – the question is why the French Encyclopedia has cited planting (wheat) and fertilizing the soil as the primary meaning?

Culture in Swedish Encyclopedias

"Culture: agriculture; originally, cultivating the earth. More general meaning: all human activities, also results of spiritual and physical activities passed on to the next generations. The more common meaning of culture is spiritual development in fields like knowledge, literature, arts and religion. In archeology, culture pertains to the remains of a certain geographical location at a given point of time."[2]

Again, as in the previous definitions, the evolutionary, virtual quality of the vital phenomenon, culture, has been conveyed through listing some of its effects: "spiritual development in fields like knowledge, literature, arts and

---

1- The Finnish Encyclopedia.
2 *Bra Bokers Lexicon.*

religion", for they are – and will always be – undoubtedly the highest ways to human evolution.

Culture in Danish Encyclopedias

"Derived from the Latin word *cultra*, culture means agricultural, development and production. Culture represents the series of processes used by human beings to change natural phenomena. In its limited meaning, culture depicts earth fertilization, raising and improving trees, production and purification of bacteria, and the results of such development.

From a broader point of view, it means all human activities – and their outcomes – whether physical or nonphysical, which are passed on to the next generation in form of social heritage, rather than genetically.

In philosophy, culture traditionally pertains to individuals, representing man's objective activities concerning himself, his environment, self-enhancement and   attaining the highest moral virtues.

Sociologically speaking, man is part of a whole. There-fore, the term "culture" should be considered in association with society. Thus, the definition for culture would be: the vast and complex series of knowledge, ideologies, arts, morals, traditions or any capability acquired by man as a member of society.[1]

Sociology basically draws a line between physical and nonphysical culture. Furthermore, it tries to combine *culture* with *society*, since it considers all human phenomena to be dependent upon social culture. Thus, social roles are to some extent determined by culture. In fact, when people are colloquially regarded as cultured, it merely means how close they are to the culture of the higher social classes, and "high or low" culture actually shows how similar peoples' culture is to 18th or 19th century European or American culture."[2]

The Danish encyclopedia's definition and description of culture brings us to several points:

1- Quoted from Edward Burnett Tylor, English anthropologist.
2- *The Gylelendals Encyclopedia.*

1. Culture is the knowledge acquired through mental and physical activities used by man in order to change his natural surroundings.

2. "In its limited meaning, culture depicts earth fertilization, raising and improving trees, production and purification of bacteria, and the results of such development."

   The phrase "limited meaning" in the above statement lacks precision. As in other dictionaries and encyclopedias, it would have been more appropriate had it been regarded as the primary, or one of the other meanings of culture.

3. The general meaning of culture includes "all human activities – and their outcomes – whether physical or nonphysical, which are passed on to the next generation in form of social heritage rather than genetically."

   This statement clearly depicts the (relative) stability of cultures – which is absolutely correct, for phenomena and activities heading for destruction cannot have a role in establishing the fundamental basics of man's virtually proper lifestyle.

4. "In philosophy, culture traditionally pertains to individuals, representing man's objective activities concerning himself, his environment, self-enhancement and attaining the highest moral virtues."

   This statement obviously approves that culture is an objective human activity pertaining to man's own self, his peers, his environment and also his self-development aiming for the highest spiritual virtues, clearly an evolutional phenomenon.

5. The sociological claim, "Man is part of a whole ..." is absolutely correct, and in approval of almost every encyclopedia published by civilized countries all around the world.

6. "Sociology ... tries to combine *culture* with *society*, considering the fact that all human phenomena are dependent upon social culture."

The point here is that, if human development and evolution had been followed as a principle throughout history, philosophical and sociological approaches would have enhanced each other, rather than fall separate.

7. One of the final statements reads, "when we speak of 'high and low' culture, we actually mean how close people's culture is to 18th and 19th century European and American culture."

The author(s) have astonishingly based the criterion for high or low culture on 18th and 19th century cultures of Europe and America, whereas other societies, e.g. Eastern countries, possess cultures much better established, more delicate and more evolutional.

Culture Seen in Turkish Reference Books

"Culture is consisted of a nation's way of thought and works of art resulted in by imitation, criticism and experiences acquired throughout life; any lifestyle caused by connecting thoughts with hearing; improving thought levels and standards of social life through criticism, appreciation, comparison and gathering necessary information."

The significant point in these statements is, "improving the level of thought and standards of social life through criticism, appreciation…"[1]

Culture is, of course, a factor in improving thoughts and social lifestyles. The point lacking attention here is the evolutional aspect of culture, which has been emphasized by almost all distinguished encyclopedias around the world.

Here are more statements on culture quoted from another Turkish reference book:

"The word "culture" found its way into the Turkish language from French and Latin after young Turks came to office in 1910, when Mustapha Kamal began vast cultural changes; it generally means civilizations remaining from the past. Its other meaning are:

These materials have been translated by Mr. Ahmadpoor. [1]

- A nation or peoples' specific cultural or civilizational change;
- One's knowledge and cultural learning;
- Purifying on element or substance of unwanted alien material;
- Biological processes in agriculture, or raising various bacteria."

Culture in the Encyclopedia of Human Rights

Culture, every human's right to contribute to cultural life, has been presented in the World Treaty on Human Rights as:

Article 1027: Every human being is entitled to the right to live freely, contribute to his society's cultural lifestyle, and enjoy its scientific and artistic advantages.

Everyone has the right to be provided with material and moral support caused by scientific endeavors or literary and artistic works.

This right has been further emphasized in the Treaty of Economic, Social and Cultural Rights.

Article 1051: All member countries of this treaty are in official agreement on these rights for every human being:

a. to contribute to cultural life;

b. to use the advantages of scientific advances and its applications;

c. to be physically and morally supported for one's scientific literary or artistic accomplishments.

Article 2015: Members of this treaty are to play an active role towards the achievement of these ends by means of developing science and culture.

Article 3015: Members of this treaty totally agree on the right of free research in scientific and creative domains.

Article 4015: All members of the treaty acknowledge the necessity of international cooperation towards scientific and cultural development.

Defending human rights against racial injustices in cultural issues has been emphasized in this treaty.

Article 5:   In accordance with the fundamental rights stated in Article 2 of this treaty, all members pledge to prevent any kind of racial injustice – whether in race, skin color, nationality or ethnic group – so that any human being can enjoy equal rights, especially in:

a. economics, particularly social and cultural rights;

b. the right to participate in cultural activities. The treaty also prohibits any kind of sexist, biased injustice or cruelty to women.

Article 13:   Membering countries are to make any effort towards dealing with socioeconomic injustices to women, so that women and men may have equal rights, particularly in sports events and all cultural activities.

The UNESCO officially undertakes the responsibility of safeguarding and supervising support and development of cultural rights. The UNESCO relies on these agreements in order to attain its goals: the UNESCO treaty on protecting cultural possessions during military invasion, approved on May 14, 1954, also known as the Hague Treaty; its protocol, May 14, 1954; the UNESCO treaty on preventing smuggling, importing or exporting cultural monuments and objects, November 14, 1970; the treaty on the protection of cultural heritage, November 16, 1972; the statement on the Principles of Cultural International Cooperation, November 14, 1966; the UNESCO statement on Principles of Satellite Transmitter Usage for Free Information flow, and Cultural Exchange, November 15, 1972 and also the UNESCO statement on Mass Media Participation and Role in Enhancing Peace and International Relationships, and Protecting Human Rights; Fighting Racial Injustice and War, November 28, 1978.

Other approved agreements aiming to protect cultural rights include an article obliging all museums to be available to all people, December 14, 1960; recommendations on preventing illegal import or export of cultural objects, November 19, 1964; recommendations on national support of cultural and natural heritage, November 16, 1972; recommendations on the protection of historical places, November 26, 1976; recommendations on the protection of contemporary historical monuments, November 28, 1978; UNESCO'S advice on the situation of artists, October 27, 1980, along with the international treaty on social and cultural rights sanctioned by the Socio-economical Commission on May 11, 1976, according to which the UNESCO is to regularly report to the commissions the progress in issues concerning its duties in the rights explained in Article 18. Information on the progress of the contents of Article 15 of the treaty – on the right to attend cultural activities – are recorded as UNESCO's economical, legal, cultural and social rights advances.[1]

Convergences of Islamic Culture and Human Rights

1. Both Islamic Culture and the Human Rights agree on items ‹a› and ‹b› for Article 1027.
2. Items ‹a›, ‹b›, and ‹c› of Article 1015 are also culturally agreed upon.
3. Likewise Articles 2015, 3015, 4015 and 5.
4. In Article 13, the two cultures do not agree in their approaches to the different rights considered for men and women.[2]

The Criterion in Islamic Culture

Any cultural phenomenon or activity opposing the highest human virtues, like morals or religion, is unacceptable in Islam. Culture, or any phenomenon or culture arising as culture in the society, which is in conflict with human dignity, and the perfectionistic tendencies in man, however attractive it may be, is prohibited by Islam.

1- *The Encyclopedia of Human Rights.*
2- For a further detailed treatise, see M.T. Ja'fari, *Universal Human Rights: From the Viewpoints of Islam and the West, pp.292-306* (also available in English https://jeyranmain.com/2017/11/08/universal-human-rights-a-comparative-research/).

This is the most important duty of a dynamic culture, which is strongly supported in Islam.

Chapter Two

The Essence of Evolutional Culture

Culture is a Bi-polar Reality (Primordial and Objective)

The bi-polar quality of culture means it possesses both primordial and objective aspects, just like the bi-polar quality of beauty does. Since conceiving beauty depends on human psychological and mental characteristics (other living beings are incapable of it), comprehending culture also has an primordial aspect resulted by "The Principle of Protecting Evolutional Essence".

As beauty has a virtually external aspect, such as the refreshing appearances of a flower, moonlight, a riverfall, or beautiful handwriting, so does culture, like observable examples of morals, works of art, and architectural characteristics representing various external acquisitions and ideals.

The most apparent evidence for the bi-polar quality of culture is the same as that of beauty, which is specifically devoting the capability of comprehending beauty to man. In other words, cultural life is exclusive to human beings. If we consider all of the given definitions for culture, we find that none are applicable to animals.

The more spiritual and nobler a culture is the more human it is.

Human perception and activities are undoubtedly unlimited from an evolutionary point of view. Man's experiences throughout history obviously prove that although no human being can innately achieve the essence of greatness, moving on a path towards the highest virtues is nevertheless a characteristic of mankind which has caused his immense accomplishments and all well-established encyclopedias around the world approve of. Hence, those activities and phenomena not rising from mental and psychological processes, cannot fit in the definition of culture, no matter how appealingly fantastic they may be. Even if interesting issues play a role in preventing life from becoming monotonous and fading the boundary between physical and spiritual affairs, they should nevertheless be excluded from culture – for the sake of the essence of culture itself – let alone when they are harmful, e.g. obscene pictures which demolish moral chastity, or some types of music and drugs. Unfortunately, fallacious paralogism has brought about deviations in the highly virtual meaning of culture, degrading it to a level which ranks humans with lowly animals, like gathering many huge snakes intrigued to bite; as ancient Persian culture states:

Scorpions do not sting out of revenge or hate; their nature causes them to do so

However, some lethally dangerous "human beings" tend to use all of their valuable capabilities and talents consciously for their own selfish pleasures and desires, reasoning that 'pain is terrible, and losing one's wealth and possessions is truly painful' This is the natural ego observed in man throughout history. Can brotherhood, equality, intelligible freedom, graciousness, and human dignity be achieved through such natural egos so deeply immersed in conflicting disturbance? By no means, for such a wish would prove only a humiliatingly deceitful hallucination. Therefore, accomplishing high virtues such as unity, logical equality and brotherhood in human societies inevitably requires perfect cultural elements like proper, meritorious morals and the highest qualities, such as justice, dutifulness, sympathy towards peers, accountability towards other fellow citizens and conceiving the exquisite glory of the universe by comprehending its beauty and fine order, all of which guide man along the quickest possible way to the creator of the rules of equality among men. No other path would lead to the pure ideal depicted by Universal Human Rights, man's general culture, morals and human universal nature.

Nowadays, scientists, experts and anyone with the least basic knowledge, can merely refer to any well-known encyclopedia to realize the essence of a culture able to save humanity, which can be defined as:

"The proper quality or deserved methods used for those of man's physical or spiritual needs based on human logical thoughts and emotions arisen from intelligible evolutionary lifestyles."

This is a fundamental part of our discussions on culture. In other words, by presenting the definitions of culture in various well-known encyclopedias all over the world, we prove – at this critical period of time – that the commonalites between them all are properness, perfection, physical and spiritual development, graciousness, dignity, integrity, meritorious life, responsible freedom, and lawful justice.

Now let us analyze the above mentioned definition[1] that we stated as the most comprehensive of all. Doing so, we will come to four main principles vital to achieving the important ends and content of culture.

The Four Principles of Culture as Drived from the Reviewed Definitions

One: The concept of culture – as presented in civilized nations – include "properness" and "deservingness" based upon the logical thoughts and emotions arisen from people. Thus, although some phenomena in some societies may be regarded as culture, they cannot even be considered as true cultural phenomena, let alone if they conflict with reasonable thinking, emotions, and literature for they do not contain logical thought or perfect human emotions. This is why no aspect of selfishness (racism, greed for money, power, fame or pleasure) can fit into the concept of culture, for as we quoted from the world's most distinguished encyclopedias:

"Culture is the proper quality or deserved method of the phenomena in man's life; in other words, culture contains the highest values."

1- That makes it 164 + 1 definitions of culture altogether.

Thus, those who call greed for fame, money, power, pleasure, selfishness or mutiny culture, have betrayed the highest of human virtues terribly. Calling a person or a society cultureless is the worst insult possible.

Two: Without culture as we defined it, human life does not deserve to go on, for a life without culture means a life empty of meaning, thought, logic or perfect human emotions.

Three: The more the culture of a society depends on logical principles and high human receptions, the more meritorious and proper it will be.

Four: Culture is a two-dimensional reality, consisting of absolute and relative aspects.

Clearly, by "absolute" we do not mean in the philosophical sense, but that it is much more comprehensive than other relative cultural elements. Such a categorization brings us to general and special cultures.

Special cultures, caused by the relative aspect of culture, pertains to certain nations or peoples of specific thoughts or emotions. A few notable examples are the cultures of bullfighting in Spain, or the exaggerated amount of courtesy and bowing in Japan.[1]

General culture pertains to meritorious qualities appropriate to man's physical or spiritual lifestyle, phenomena and activities not limited to any specific nation or race, e.g. cultures like aesthetics, mutual respect among people, justice, knowledge, and creating heroes.

We may conclude from the above statements that, since culture means the proper qualities fit for the physical or spiritual phenomena and activities in man's life, accepting and reflecting the totally natural compulsory facts or effects of human life – such as eating and drinking – cannot be regarded as a part of

---

[1] - Such inordinate cultures – like other special cultural elements and phenomena – are heading for demise, except for principle–based cultural aspects.

culture; however, their connection to prayers, which is quite common in Islam and some other religious societies, fits into the domain of culture. Defending one's life, preparing a shelter, or accessing scientific or philosophical facts through the senses can also be considered as a part of culture.

The Connection between the Necessary Cultural Elements and the Merited Ones

It is quite difficult to make a clear distinction between these two types of cultural elements without encountering a conflict, for accusing man of ignoring the gloriously perfect human ideals for providing the necessities of his life, would be denying the most obvious of fact – all reason and conscience.

Defying human glory and man's great ideals, and degrading mankind down to being equivalent to honeybees, means destroying all humanity. Furthermore, isolating cultural concepts from the vital facts of life – like knowledge, science and other mental activities that adjust or life – leads to the separation of perfectionist tendencies from normal life, which in turn causes spiritual dilemma between "natural and evolutionarily spiritual" life.

Early in the 21st century, we have seen many pioneer societies on the earth making great effort in order to implement the most realistic economic, social, legal or moral ideologies in their communities. Not only did they fail to do so, but they have even – as we have already seen in the definitions of culture in such countries as Russia or China – clearly admitted the necessity of a pioneer spiritual culture regardless of any presumptions of an ideology. Accepting the necessity of culture is not brought about by one or a few conventional factors, but by man's human nature, without man would totally lose his humanity – when "man stepped which out of his prehistoric caves and entered the unfeeling wheels of a machine."

Hence, ever since man came to being, he had culture beside him to provide his life with delicacy and fulfill his highest spiritual ideals. Man's close connection with culture has given profound cultural value to morals and arts (in a general sense), true knowledge, "taboo morals", customs and even laws. It is quite a simple, unquestionable fact that without spiritual culture[1], man would lose his life.

Solzhenitsyn[2] has thus elaborated on this matter at the International Congress of Philosophy in Liechtenstein:

"We can generalize the same moral expectations we consider for man to governments, rulers, parliaments and political parties. If politics does not have a moral basis, there will truly be no future for mankind. Russians have been literally witnessing this since centuries ago. I unfortunately see that my countries' goals have fallen way behind even the West. After seventy years of unbelievable pressure and suffocating dictatorship, there is now abundant freedom among the poor classes, and many people have totally forsaken their conscience; however, we must not let this problem distribute among other countries. As we approach the end of the second millennium, this problem continues to threaten all of mankind."

The Progress Crisis

He adds:

"We do make progress – but in what? What kind of advances are the issue here? Progress is limited to technological civilization, more luxury in life and military explorations. We are voraciously swallowing the nature that we take for granted. But among such progress – devoid of any moral development – our physical needs increase with such extreme rapidity that we are left confused. We insatiably keep expanding our possessions [in other words, we more and more use up our resources of human identity]; however, when it comes to acquiring higher moral virtues and spiritual goals, we prove to be futile tools of greedy exploitations. Transportation and communications now take place at incredible

---

1- Spiritual culture includes a) high moral virtues, b) art, as an indication of man's deepest emotions concerning "what should be done", c) freedom – in the sense of having the power of choice, which arises in actively powerful qualities during evolution, and d) religion, addressing questions such as: "Who am I? Where have I come from? Why am I here? Where will I end up?"

2- Russian writer, who greatly criticized the Soviet Union from a mystical – religious point of view.

ease; people can travel all around the world with a mere pressing of a television button.

Yet, in the middle of such an ocean of superficial information, the human soul is not only failing to progress, but is actually heading for doom. The more materialistically luxurious man becomes, the more will his spiritual life fade away. Scientific, technological, and economic advances are leading us to slavery. Constantly in seek of new discoveries, we have lost our goals; what indeed, is the end in life? We failed to escape from our endless responsibilities. Telephones and television demolished the integrity of our time, and began to impose the conditions upon us. Communication among humans began to frail. People, particularly the elderly, found themselves living alone. Unable to put technology to use in welfare aims or to unite humans, we have become its plaything. Progress couldn't keep us away from globalizing responsibilities. Furthermore, we are increasingly unprepared for them. We have lost the rhythm that was always alongside our virtual and physical well-being; good and evil have become illusively obscured.

Another outcome of our spiritual degradation is the absence of the relaxed attitude we used to have towards death. However financially secure one may be, the fear of death starts a cold sweat on any tycoon's skin. Insatiable, scandalous lifestyles have brought about an immense horror of death. As man gradually tries to consider himself the center of the universe, he tends to see the universe as a part of himself, rather than see himself as a part of the universe.

The presumption "Everything leads to death" has begun to dominate us like a threatening weapon. Nuclear threats ruled the twentieth century. Although everything seemed indifferent afterwards, the threat created a uniting concept in order to impose itself again on Western societies. Towards the end of the century, internal ideological decay caused Communism to self-destruct. The demise of Communism caused the nuclear threat to recede, at an unpredictably rapid rate. The world, however, still does not feel completely secure.

Communism still lives on in some parts of the former Soviet Union, for as brutal capitalism continues to disgustingly ravage its national resources – to such an extent that even has the West astonished – Communist slogans on 'equality and justice in poverty' have appealed to classes unable to withstand the conditions."[1]

Has the Reality Called Culture Undergone Evolution throughout Historic Changes?

Progress in several cultural elements, such as science, cultivating talents and potentials, usually responds with a positive answer: Yes, culture has evolved throughout history. Of course, evolutional progress in culture is any perfectionist human being's ideal. But does history also confirm such progress?

If development means scientific advances concerning nature and human lifestyles, such culture has definitely made profound progress. The reason is quite obvious: the vital needs of life in nature, and also man's greed and ambition for power has greatly expanded the necessary phenomena of culture.

We have already noted in our definition of culture that the necessities and worthy aspects of cultures do not always necessarily arise from reality, for man has time and again created artificial demands out of his selfish greed for power, and labeled them the necessities of life. For instance, exploitations, weakening peoples' will power and various sexual intrigues have been called art, considered a meritorious culture.

However, the other aspect of culture – including man's evolutionary needs for perfection – despite an ideal to any clear conscience, has not only failed to progress, but even shrunk due to advances in man's necessities for natural life (i.e., physical culture), to such an extent that it is sometimes considered as a disturbing factor. Let us consider the reasons why physical culture has made so much progress, but evolutionary culture heads for deterioration (of course, we do not intend to deny any exceptional cases):

1. Inability in finding a culture that can moderate selfishness and protect and follow evolutionary virtues.

1- *The Kayhan*, Friday, October 6, 1995.

2. Affections that lead to positive virtues vanish due to the ignorance of cultures receiving intelligible and observable beauty.
3. Neglecting cultures concerning rights, power and how to use power in order to uphold righteousness.
4. Ignoring the culture of benefiting from outstanding figures and genius among the society.
5. Greed for power, fame and wealth has demolished man's culture of scientific conscience, except for a painfully meager minority in which it has been confined inside their pure souls.
6. What on earth happened to the constructive culture that could elevate human relationships from a hide-and-seek charade to an ocean of pure souls where waves constantly meet?

Human spirit is a unified soul, whereas in animals it is but a rigid lump of clay.

* * * *

Their numbers are in the likeness of waves: the wind will have brought them into number (into plurality from unity).

* * * *

Inasmuch as God sprinkled His light upon them (mankind), (they are essentially one): His light never becomes separated (in reality) (Rumi, Masnavi, Book 2).

* * * *

7. After all these years of endeavor to create civilizations and humanities, and all the toil and sacrifice put into making fundamentals – like a) meritorious life, b) human grace and dignity, c) intelligible, responsible freedom and d) total equality towards laws – a reality, not only puppet rulers today still unconsciously do obey powerful tyrants totally ignorant of humanity, but philosophical cultures such as Machiavellian's doctrines on survival and the theories of authoritarians like Hobbes or Nitche are even taught at universities

without the least criticism. There are dozens of other examples verifying evolutionary meritorious cultures being are ignored by the majority of today's human society.

Among the worst effects of the decline in meritorious evolutionary cultures on man's life was his deprivation of acquiring higher virtual truth, which led to committing any kind of injustice. As a result, their perception of reality has become extremely limited. Let us consider an example of such intense limitation:

- People have lost their ability to comprehend mental intelligible beauties. Mechanized life culture prevented man from understanding the beauty lying in the universe and in the essence of life. In other words, man is now only capable of sensing the beauty of a flower (an observable beauty) – that is how painfully degraded mechanized life has made him.

  Thus, the beauty of realities like justice, righteousness, freedom of conscience, human dignity, and chastity and the essence of life remain buried in books of sermons.

- Various greed-driven crimes defying all morals and conscience, especially in political cultures, have caused irreversible damage to evolutionary culture.

- The changes occurring in the logics behind human socioeconomic trends – shifting towards increasingly consumerist societies requiring more and more manufacture – has demolished the culture of "earn to live", which leads us to "live to provide the desires of the greedy" culture:

  "In today's technological circumstances, the motto has become: More Production, Better Economy!"

  Do they really not know – or do they consciously ignore – who is actually responsible for more production? Are they unaware of those trampled under the pressure of manufacture increases? They do not seem to realize at all that however plentiful the mines and resources on earth may be, they will eventually run out.

- Racism and regionalism are other "meritorious evolutionary anti-cultures" that are rapidly strengthening along with the "development of today's civilizations". In fact, unlike many short-living socioeconomic theories and schools of thought, racism and regionalism are rooting stronger day by day, putting all laws, cultures, knowledge, economics, and universal human power up to ridicule.

Disharmonious Cultural Elements in Real Facts May Demolish All of Human Culture

We have already mentioned that since man is directly involved in the formation of culture – it is man who builds up a culture out of his environment, historical phenomena, relative and/or absolute ideals and his concept of ideology, and also it is man who attempts to harmonize permanent laws with temporary events in a period of time in order to create a culture he could live by, and finally because man has too many aspects to harmonize – cultural elements usually suffer from disharmony, and ruling authorities prefer accountable "things" rather than "people".

The primary reason for such disharmony is the authoritarian and power-greedy tendencies that prefer cultural elements directly or indirectly effective in enhancing domination and power. Thus, there would be no need for any organized system of social culture. In other words, it is possible to have a moral culture based on emotions and still base scientific culture on purely mental anthropology. Like-wise, having abstract tendencies in ethical artistic cultures, and yet seeing observable tendencies in its historical culture is also possible. Or maybe a purely supernatural religious culture beside a totally realistic scientific culture, e.g. European Christianity during the last two centuries compared to their scientific realism.

The reason behind the destructive effect of disharmony of cultural elements upon the entire Islamic culture lies in the unity of human life, primarily based on "man's evolutionary virtues." When basic cultural elements fail, unity vanishes and all of human culture faces certain doom. The most harmful form of disharmony in cultural elements is the isolation of spiritual basics and mental human virtues from physical aspects of culture, which is a result of greed for wealth, power, and purely animal-like desires.

Here is an excerpt from a paper by Paul G. Bahanan, anthropology professor at the University of California:

> *"All cultures undergo change, some slowly and some rapidly. Since culture consists of various factors, changes in one of them would also affect the others. Some sociologists believe that many social problems are due to disharmonious changes in cultural elements. Cultural retardation occurs when some parts of a culture tend to follow others.*
> *Many cultural retardations in the history of the United States have occurred in its non-physical traditions, thoughts and issues. Science and technology advance so rapidly that they have put spiritual issues way behind."*[1]

Reasons for Disharmony in Social Cultural Elements

The main reasons citable for disharmony in the cultural elements of a society are:

1. **Egotism of the rulers:** No meritorious reality in the world has survived destructive influences by the selfish. When people believe that "law" is a spider web aimed to entrap the meek, culture will indeed be regarded as devoid of any worthy qualities of life or compulsory guidelines.

2. **Hedonism,** which arises with "the natural self" and strengthens with **nihilism**, and defies all laws and principles.

3. **Authoritarianism**, in any form or caused by anyone it may be, demolishes all cultural merits, and so cleverly decorates their remains that it seems to claim, "I have granted you the most desirable culture you could imagine!" Poor simpletons who never cease to be

---

[1]- *The World Book Encyclopedia.*

deceived time and again by jargon like cultural or civilizational transfer.

The road is smooth, and under it are pitfalls: amidst the names there is a dearth of meaning.

Words and names are like pitfalls: the sweet (flattering) word is the sand for (the sand that sucks up) the water of our life. (Rumi, Masnavi, Book One: 160-1061).

Shorter Definition of Culture

Decoration and collage of every phenomenon of human life is proportionate to the value that a society gives to that very phenomenon that has its own origin in the deep feelings of the people who live in that society.

Then, every culture is consisted of two elements:

First Element: human life phenomena comprise the realities related with man and the world, and specific human facts like the necessary affairs for natural life, science, art, religion, ethics, law, politics, worldview and so on and so forth. These affairs in view of their causes and basic persuasions are not essentially described as culture, because each one of them is an independent necessary cause whether it is endorsed by our inner feellings or not these affairs are affirmated as effects. Food, cloth, housing, medication, and even science, law, politics, and the like, which all have their origin in the essential causes are not cultural phenomena as such, rather they are all decorated and painted with the values of a particular culture.

Second Element: the value that is signaled by decoration and painting of the phenomena with the deep feelings of a society. The ethics of nations in cultures originates from this second element. For the elementary and secondary materials of human inner feelings in every society are concerned with the particular geographical and environmental factors, mental coordinates, historical background, and the principles that they have chosen for thee explication of the basic quadruple relations (human relations with oneself, world, God, and fellow human beings).

It is needless to say that the second element of culture is its very essence. If we look with more precision we would know that the foundation of movement and evolution or continuation of the historical identity of a nation is this very element of the culture: i.e. decoration and painting of human life phenomena with deep human perceptions and emotional persuasions.

After providing a short definition of culture we turn to the basic classification of culture. Culture can be divided into two types of follower and pioneer in view of the two major sides involved in the very phenomenon of culture, i.e. 1- man, 2- the feelings governing the values that decorate life.

This division can be applied to all cases where the oughts can decorated by values: e.g. follower law, pioneer law, follower ethics, pioneer ethics, follower politics, pioneer ethics.

The follower culture, as the phrase itself suggests to one's mind, is an effect of free and uncommitted activities of humanity. This type of culture does not have anything to do with the noble ideals and goals of human life as the same is the case with the follower law that does not pay any attention to ideals and goals. Likewise in the follower ethics man cannot take any concrete step towards the fulfilment of the noble ideals.

The only thing that can assist humanity in the path of true evolution is the pioneer culture.

Chapter Three

The Pursuing and Pioneering Culture

Upon a necessary study of the long life story of various nations, one finds two general types of culture: The Pursuing and Pioneering Culture

"Pioneering culture refers to physical or non-physical qualities and ways of life based on no pre-established principle, but seeking approval only through people's desires."

In other words, such cultures arise from any need, behavior or desire people have, regardless of their compliance with man's non-physical realities.

Thus, any of people's desires opposing religion, morals, dignity, or logic can be considered as culture! Such Fraudulence in the name of culture[1] has greatly spread during our times, and will undoubtedly lead to the annihilation of humanity. Although Pursuing and Pioneering Culture obviously means obeying human desires, we must keep in mind that it also provides selfish authoritarians with the chance they need.

In fact, this kind of culture both satisfies people's purely natural desires, and those of their rulers, who find the opportunity to not only fulfill their people's wishes, but also disguise any factors opposing religion, morals, or human dignity in the name of culture.

Follower laws could prove to be much more suitable for people's needs rather than follower culture, for "laws" pertain directly to the context of people's lifelines, which thus can be constantly modified and adjusted according to people's actual needs; culture, on the other hand, being based on non-physical beauties and delicacies, cannot be manipulated by people's physical needs. However, any lowly, morality-defying activity or quality is nowadays publicized in the name of culture.

---

1 - At times, these selfish imposters even have their intellectual-looking directors add the term "free" to culture in order to optimize its deceiving affects: 'free culture!"

Considering this theory proposed by several sociologists, we may come to the conclusion that a constructive, pioneer culture as the leader of human civilization should be a doctor, not a waiter:

"Doctors are highly different from waiters. Waiters in a restaurant provide you with whatever you desire, whereas a doctor follows his own academic principles; he prescribes what he believes necessary, regardless of what you think. A pioneer politician should be like a doctor, not a waiter."

Whenever Man Has Followed Pioneer Systems, He Has Successfully Made Progress

Let us present a few examples to elaborate on this critical point:

a. Is it possible for an ordinary person to interfere in the most advanced of academic issues merely by having freedom and Pursuing and Pioneering Culture?

b. Can the medical practice allow an uneducated person to examine and cure sick people only on premises of freedom and follower culture?

c. Can we possibly let anyone enter an operation room and, relying simply on freedom and culture, begin to cut up people's bodies?

d. Is it possible to conceive someone stepping into a gun factory and start to comment on everything, and meddle with any tool he wishes, on the basis that, "I am making use of freedom and follower culture?, of course. The times when people were deprived of freedom and their desired culture are over. Decadence is forbidden all over the world!"

e. Will there ever be a day when anyone would comment on any scientific or technological matter he wished, and if told, "You are not educated in such issues, so you should not meddle or interfere", he would retort, "Yes, I am entitled to use my own culture and freedom, for the age of decadent deceptions and forcing people to imprison their thoughts are over!"

f. Culture and freedom are indeed amazing. Consider someone whimsically wearing a decorated military uniform. If he faces protest, can he claim, "Down with the anti-liberty! Down with the anti-culture!"

Obviously, all of the above-mentioned who carry the book entitled *Freedom*[1] should be taken to mental asylums.

Now we can move on to the main point: whenever man has considered an issue essential to his survival, he has applied pioneer principles – sciences concerning human relationships, managing laborers to one's own advantage, social leadership, political activities, and employing cultures for specific purposes, medicine, surgery, lethal arms and armor and military propaganda – quite successfully, though man's intrinsic progress calls for the truths about his perfectionist growth.

Hence, all the cries for freedom, free follower culture, and free art! And humanity was degraded back to even before the prehistoric ages. The reason why is that cavemen had not confined their potential for progress to their own selfish desires, and had – consciously or unconsciously – begun to activate their talents.

Here are a few examples of the culture of facts demolished in many societies – not because they failed to resist and satisfy man's evolution, but due to selfish rulers making illusive brainwashing using terms like freedom, free culture, free arts and other deceiving magic tricks:

1. Culture as authentic sympathy for our fellow human beings, not a business tool;
2. authentically moral consciences guiding our souls towards the highest goals of life, like a precise compass;
3. culture, the highest aim in life;
4. culture depicting honesty and keeping promises only for its moral desirability, not for making a profit;
5. culture in the form of responsible freedom and just deeds and thoughts;
6. culture as the sacred identity for knowledge;
7. culture in the form of cooperation in making use of various forces, which are blessings;

1- "Freedom" is the name of a book by the English philosopher John Stuart Mill, concerning freedom of speech, thought, deed and writing – though without ade-quate logical care. Although it includes interesting points, sensible freedom and addressing immoral behaviors which allows people to do whatever they desire in the name of freedom have been ignored.

8. culture as the generalization of constructive, pioneer arts;
9. culture as referring to the media, documented propaganda, avoiding lies, and misinterpreting the truth;
10. culture as the highest of cultures, providing all people with their deserved earnings.

Our statement, "Whenever man has followed pioneer systems, he has successfully achieved progress" does not imply that man can evolve progressively by abstracting and adjusting a group of key issues called laws; we mean to state that throughout history, whenever man has made and obeyed laws based on well-prepared information – without the influence of public desires – he has made successful evolution. Thus, in issues concerning science, technology, and any matters benefiting man's physical needs or selfish desires, we see man successfully using pioneer culture, whereas in evolving the essence of man – which involves religion and morals – he has totally ignored pioneer culture, and followed cultural phenomena in the name of "following free culture."

Categorization of Cultures

Cultures Can Be Categorized into Four Main Groups:

1. **Sedimentary culture**: In this form of culture, fixed laws based on ethical, mental, geographical, and historical factors form totally unchangeable lifestyles and guidelines which can destroy or adapt other changes to their own advantage. If nonhuman and non-natural factors cause a sedimentary culture, compulsory environmental factors or the people's psychological incapabilities to adjust to positive changes may lead to useless insisting on "self"-orientated activities.

2. **"Colorless liquid"** culture refers to deceptions and explanations based on no fundamental, psychological roots, which are hence constantly variable. Societies possessing a history, of course, seldom seem "colorlessly liquid", for as we have already seen, culturalism originates from a basically active psychological source.

Any society throughout history tends naturally to pass its concepts and guidelines in life on to the next generations, and while this phenomenon – or better said, psychological factor – remains, the culture will also keep its stability in a number of activities and effects.

Thus we now come to two points:

a. As we have already mentioned in our discussion on Cultural Disharmony and Its Reasons,[1] there is no logical need for the cultural elements of a society to by harmoniously related; therefore, some elements may be "liquid," rootless and highly change-prone, while others are stable and well-established. In some Arab societies, for instance, stable moral cultures accompany fervid changes in political cultures.

b. Despite being a relatively stable phenomenon, and however constructive a culture may usually be, when based on Machiavellian rules of social life management, they will fade away. We also know that despite all of the immense advances man has made, he is becoming increasingly powerless in distinguishing "means and ends", particularly in societies incapable of managing human power; in such societies, power dominates people, and their essential culture destroys any principle or culture aiding them to achieve their goals.

3. Egotist culture (follower egotism): In this kind of culture, activities and effects that interpret cultural facts are essentially the desired ones, and completely quench cultural ideals. Such "self-orientation" specifically pertains to 19th and 20th - century scientific, technological and economic cultures.

"The egotist" inhibits the main identity of culture, which is creativity and developing the ideals of the "human self" in various aspects of life. The other effect of "self-orientated" culture – which is by no means less dangerous than the first – is changing man from the creator of science and technology to a helpless part of them. We should keep in mind that when one or several aspects of human life – for example, the art of make-up – turns "egotist", it would become unable to

---

- See P. 112.[1]

satisfy other culture-seeking aspects – e.g., the desire for truth. Therefore, duality in character arises; the ego partly mixed with the effect (in this case make-up techniques) dissolves in it, for it has turned " egotist", and the other, seeing the rest of the human culture-seeking aspects fade away, gradually disappears, and the whole character is engulfed by the original effect.

Fortunately, observations show that not many people are obsessed by "egotist" influences, so there are always people conscious enough to condemn other's infatuation by some qualities in life or the weakening of other human culture-seeking aspects. Alexis Carl in 20th century France, Thomas Eliot in England and William James in America – and also many other scholars from all over the world – have openly denounced such internal captivities.

4. Dynamic, objective and pioneer culture: The following verses depict the pure source this kind of culture originates form:

Generations have passed away, and this is a new generation: the moon is the same moon, the water is not the same water.

The justice is the same justice, and the learning is the same learning too; but those generations and peoples have been changed (supplanted by others).

Generations on generations have gone, O sire, but these Ideas (Divine attributes) are permanent and everlasting.

The water in this channel has been changed many times: the reflexion of the moon and of the stars remains unaltered.

Therefore its foundation is not in the running water; nay, but in the regions of the breadth (wide expanse) of Heaven (Rumi, Masnavi, Book Six, 3175-3179).[1]

This kind of culture is not affected by activities susceptible to the variables and unstable aspects of life, for it is caused by

---

[1]- Mowlavi is implying by "the highest of heavens" in fact the fundamentals of the creation of the universe which is linked to the human soul:

Indeed, it was you who bonded the circle of the universe.

permanent natural facts and originally human aspects, and aims for the relative ideals guiding man towards the highest goal in life. In fact, this is definitely the human culture that is essential to any human civilization throughout history. This is the culture that can free itself from greedy, selfish rulers and continue serving society.

Its other quality is its ability to neutralize morals and traditions based on imperfect thoughts, efforts to fill the realistic gaps of life, and in general, all unstably regional factors devoid of authentic ideals.

By further studying creative, objective, and pioneer cultures, we understand why many other human cultures have diminished. The main reason is the sedimentary activities caused by the deterioration of their creators, or "egotist" cultures in which man imprisons himself instead of any analyzing and explaining his activities. Therefore, even if the cultural results they cause are able to survive, they will gradually turn taboo, and disappear from the horizon of the society.

What Causes an Objective Pioneer Culture?

We must first bring back to mind the culture-seeking factor cited in the four definitions before addressing the roots of objective culture.

The general history of mankind, scientific evidence and philosophical experiences all prove that man cannot remain satisfied with his compulsory natural and biological qualities (as bees or ants do), and when his basic physical needs have been provided, he will strive to know the "hows and whys" of nature, turning his whole environment upside down to find his answers; and since his sensory, logical and mental viewpoints are unlimited, after achieving each goal he asks himself, "Now what?"

Taking such adventurous, insatiable behavior towards various situations into close consideration brings us to a basic reason (or reasons), without which we would never be able to comprehend the motives behind objective – or even other – cultures. It would be impossible to find out the factors causing the rise, climax, demise, fall, or even transfer of cultures between societies without taking the roots of culture seeking into consideration. Likewise, we would not be able to achieve a pioneer, objective culture.

Roots of Cultural Sense in Humanity

Human culture seeking appears to be based on primary and secondary factors:

THE FIRST ROOT is the active psychological factor arousing man to build and arrange his natural, physical surroundings and adjust the unchangeable phenomena around him in a way appropriate to his creative self.

THE SECOND ROOT refers to internal and external factors belonging to specific countries or peoples, which determines the former root, and explains their modes of life.

Considering the first – and primary – root of culture seeking, we may conclude that cultural diversity is as numerous as those of human aspects aiding man to adjust and change the world according to his ideals. However, we have already seen that man is not capable of building a perfect culture that would satisfy all of his various aspects; he cannot accumulate and organize all different cultural components. Unfortunately, every civilization throughout history has had to suffer such failures.

The reason for the above-mentioned inability is not due to negligence or uncontrollable inhibitions blocking the culture-makers' way, but lack of attention to the active psychological factor aiming to both build a suitable home out of natural, unchangeable processes, and cause positive changes. On the other hand, we should remember that confining a society to – for instance – its ancient monuments, does not suit today's dynamic trends. Also, how can a bundle of taboo behaviors established ages ago – with or without good reason – be able to satisfy today's highly developed man? Indeed, such arts, morals, beliefs, and lifestyles can play an active role in today's culture in two ways:

First: Their general social and/or psychological impact – if they have caused any.

Secondly: Historical application and understanding how lifestyles of the past were colored by those cultural affects, and also how the society found its definite path, the perfect "home" its people had made.

In order to have an authentically original culture, we must relate all of our ideal activities and/or outcomes to the active psychological factor, which – although stably creative– can provide them all. It would prove totally infertile, however, without being saturated with the crystal-clear viewpoint arising from man's internal, perfect culture for life.

We had better now elaborate briefly on the clear aspect of culture.

Culture's Clear and Observable Aspects

The observable aspect of culture refers to those ideas, ideals, and accounts of life materialized by visible effects in our world, e.g. works of art, moral ethics, or technology supplying our requirements.

The clear aspect of culture depicts the ideals, emotions, morals, and goals chosen for man's life, which – consciously or unconsciously – account for his individual or social lifestyle. They are "clear", which means they have no visibly observable aspect. For instance, when a French historian writes about Napoleon Bonaparte from a clearly racist point of view, he would definitely call him the greatest hero of all time, as an Iranian racist historian would do so with Xerxes in a clearly racist approach.

Assessing *The History of Gibbon* on the rise and fall of the Roman Empire, Whitehead also believes that:

"Gibbon has produced a successful account of history, albeit from a totally 19th century point of view."

Ever since the eighteenth century, the scientific aspect of culture has in two ways brought about the current situation in the West through intensive brainwashing:

First: an incredible, human reality – the eagerness for discovering facts – that has been a human ideal ever since the earliest times: science. As it

	provides men contact with facts, science is considered a critical virtue of life, thus engulfing all mental endeavors around the world.
Second:	science gave birth to technology, which caused great luxury in people's lives. Societies where technology was developing became so fascinated with its economical and prestigious advantages that, not only did they totally forget humanity and a deserved human life, they even made science a slave of its own creation, technology – "scientific bankruptcy"[1] arose, and logical human virtues were totally ignored. A clear aspect of "We are the highest race" and "We are Pioneers of Human Development" was engraved in their minds! It is now still spreading at full strength.

The unbelievable result is, the motto "I have technology, so I am the greatest on earth; I own everything all over the world, which I may use at will!"

This, indeed, is the culture that is gradually destroying original, worthy cultures of different peoples, and has clearly turned into an anti-culture.

The great cultural aspects that have been sacrificed by the clear "We are the greatest" aspect are: the highest of human emotions, a broad scope of life, the high aim of life, sympathy, and balancing powers and privileges to man's benefit. It has revived the fight for survival, which thousands of prophets, wise men, philosophers and any other human-loving person all around the world tried so hard to uproot.[2]

- Jean-Pierre Rosseau, *The History of Science*.[1]

2- You may have heard Ernest Renan's idea, "The West is the employer race, and the East the employee. That is why nature produces a larger amount of labor force!" See how this so-called "intellectual" ⇨ ruthlessly insults nature. Mr. Renan apparently knows nothing about Eastern civilizations, the true creators of science and technology. He adds, "The Western mind is industrial, official and civilizational, whereas that of the Eastern is emotional mediocre, and lacking for today's high thoughts!" It is quite surprising how such a "scholar" can be so ignorant of Eastern civilization history, and that the human brain has not changed in any race for at least 40,000 years. Most astonishing of

Various Clear Aspects of Culture

The clear, unobservable aspects of culture – which account for its observable ones – differ widely in nature, range, and activity:

1. The nature of some clear aspects of culture – which can also explain its visible aspects – arise from natural human qualities, like selfishness, greed for power, etc, each of which vary greatly in form and approach. Since they are human-originated, their range is much stronger and greater, or as Thomas Hobbes claims, "Man can attack man like a wolf." We must keep in mind, however, that all conscious individuals or communities aware of humanitarian sacrifices made in benefit of human justice and emotion throughout history, not only do not admit being affected by – and accepting – selfish and power-greedy aspects, they even pretend to be against them.

2. Racism and inadvertent patriotism, (in any way, not illogical patriotism) is another clear aspect of culture that is – consciously or unconsciously – influencing other aspects.

3. General ideals all well-balanced humans have agreed on throughout history, such as science, arts, civilization, health care, etc.

These clear aspects, if activated without being contaminated by selfishness or ambitiousness, can be – in their true nature – extremely useful. But unfortunately, as we have already mentioned, they have caused sidekicks which have totally demolished their creators' good name.

Saving ourselves from such clear aspects – which first entice us with their attractive appearances, and then turn into oceans of selfishness and greed to drown us – is only possible through determining the greatest of goals in life and adhering to them.

---

all, he didn't even try to reason inductively that most inventions have also been achieved by accident, not accurate calculations.

How to Improve the Clear Aspects of Culture and Make Them in Line with the Observable Aspects

Although the simplest and most straightforward, the way to improve the clear aspects of culture is also the most exclusive and essential one proposed by wise intellectuals. It is, however, the longest and most complicated, too.

The most direct, simplest, and still the longest and most complex way is for man to return to himself; today's man has fallen greatly astray from his own self.

Clear aspects, of culture, interpreting and explaining all cultural effects and activities are like glasses with colored lenses, changing man's viewpoint of his life. These aspects of life can undoubtedly give no pure reflection of man's observable world, for reflected observable phenomena cannot be more effective than their real image; purely imagining beauty is never as influential as seeing real, visible beauty. The imagination is only intrigued when the viewer wants to possess the beauty, or paint a picture of a beautiful phenomenon.

Likewise, a mental image of freedom cannot be as intriguing as real freedom; it can only be effective when it proves its desirability to the imaginer.

Therefore, we must distinguish clear aspects of culture from pure imagination; in order to do so, we have to consider the fact that clear aspects have the activating effect reflections and imaginations are devoid of. Besides, reflections and imaginations identically reflect what exists in the visible world – like a mirror – but they ignore their relationships with each other or basic goals fundamental factors; the clear aspect, however, accounts for all observable facts along with their connections with logical ends.

Hence, all dimensions of life – pleasure, pain, knowledge, need, logic, imagination, morality, religious and ideological tendencies, artistic creativity, etc. – are explained by the clear aspects of culture. If they are confined to facts formed by compulsory, thoughtless activities, they would in fact only be reflections acting on naturally-originated factors.

We may conclude that, in order to provide satisfactory answers to the "hows and whys" of life, the clear aspects of life should provide man's highest ideals in life. Thus, we can state that any culture unable to determine the highest aim of life, will also definitely fail to provide its ideals.

Without activating the constructive aspects of life, the highest aim of life would not be capable of being creative or dynamic. Any individual or society requires evolutionary goal-setting – whatever its cultural effects may be – in order to achieve an objective freedom which can ensure the survival of an original culture. In such cases, any cultural effect or activity would prove devoid of any saturation by idealism or providing a basis, like a heap of compulsory activities. Aimless works of art, despite being highly attractive and exquisite, can only motivate us momentarily, but they do not guide us after we are aroused. If we accept the necessity of objectivity in original cultures, the rigid traditionalism in some cultures would definitely turn into original, constructive ones.

Cultures move towards their goals just like souls do. In fact, the culture of a society depicts its soul, and all of its cultural activities and affects represent the attitude of its spirit.

Thus, the only way to create an original, objective culture is to enhance the emotions and thoughts of the members of the society, and make them so harmonious that each human being would freely be able to create his/her own desired culture.

As we have already mentioned, without elevated goals, it is impossible to achieve true freedom of character, otherwise, society would fall into "free" slovenly culturelessness, which would shatter away when compared with other cultures. Now that we have realized the need for explaining and interpreting the highest reasons and goals of life, we should find an ideology capable of such interpretations vital for creating an original, objective culture.

Ever since the earliest times, many ideologies have proposed various ideas on the highest aim of life; however, by studying them, we come to a universally agreed conclusion: "Any target is located higher than the one that is aiming at it." Thus the aim of life must be much higher than the mortal phenomena and activities of everyday life in order to provide a satisfactory explanation for the whole fundamentals of life.

Tendencies to move towards higher goals will certainly prove incompatible with the rise or fall of some cultural effects and/or activities; furthermore, the cause-and-effect rule puts culture – the "effect" – into the right evolutionary course. Of course, there is great debate over what the great aim should be, and we do not tend to go into its complicated details.

With the exception of hedonists and nihilists, all schools of thought – as we have already mentioned – agree that "the target is always higher than one aiming at it." Thus, no school of thought can present phenomenon or activities as the highest goal to make an original culture – or as Mowlana Jalal-ildin calls them, the "shadows of life":

The deliciousness of milk and honey is the reflexion of the (pure) heart: from that heart the sweetness of every sweet thing is derived.
Hence the heart is the substance, and the world is the accident: how should the heart's shadow (reflexion) be the object of the heart's desire?(Rumi, Masnavi, Book Three: 2265-2266).

The most valuable and greatest quality of objective culture seeking an objective life is its logical organization of cultural elements – the highest human ideal. Objectiveness leads to cultural organization, as having an aim for one's soul causes mental order and discipline.

It should not be so surprising to us that cultural elements suffer from so great disorder in most human societies today, for philosophers and intellectuals have also for some time claimed to be unable to determine the true aim of life. After all, when the human spirit is mutilated by economists, lawyers, psychologists, expert sociologists, and greedy technologists, how can we expect a culture with logically organized elements?!

All in all, we are left with no choice but to first solve the puzzle of the aim of life, and then move on to organizing the fundamentals and rules of a culture. Culture-maker today are apparently obliged to consider the highest aim of life; otherwise, the way today's mechanical lifestyles and uncalculated civilizations are going on, they will undoubtedly face nihilism.

The Highest Aim of Life Makes Original, Objective Cultures

No aim can suitably explain a certain period of human life – his lifetime – including all regional and social, factors depending on historical knowledge and human capabilities without addressing these four questions: Who am I? Who am I with? Where am I going to? Why am I here?

By such questions, man undoubtedly intents to find out how he depends on his world. Now matter how his ideology may be, it is enough for man to have a world to be born in, get familiar with, develop a passion for, and finally die.

Without love to explain our relationships with the world we live in, there would never be any of the vast, fascinating cultures that have formed throughout history, nor any of the arts originating from man's far-reaching ambitions. Perfectionist, ambitious man, always reaching for higher positions – however highly accomplished his activities may be – can only be saturated by divine attractions – to which the only way of entrance is the human soul – unless, however, cultural activity or effect is exaggerated and disguised so greatly that it would satisfy man's insatiable spirit. Such cultures would prove alive, colorless, sedimentary and egotist.

Considering our above discussions, we come to the conclusion that it is impossible to achieve a dynamic culture without religious and ideological factors caused by objective life.

By "ideological factors" we do not mean a heap of illogical, unverifiable beliefs, but man's spiritual awareness moving on the path of evolution towards divine attraction. As Iqbal Lahouri says:

What is religion? Rising from the earth, to achieve self-awareness of the soul.

Along such a path, the world has been resembled to man's precious body, full of both cultural results and activities to "decorate" the home. In fact, the precious "home" is the world inside the "self", which will stay with us forever; it is not a place to stay for some time and then leave.

The Culture Islam Established [1]

The culture established by Islam is an aimed life that strongly activates human aspects of aestheticism, desire for knowledge, logic, and idealism, and organizes all cultural elements. It does not isolate scientific culture from high human morals, does not separate artistic culture from the culture of economic guidance, and finally, considers the unity of culture as a dependant upon unity in human souls, thus preventing its destruction. The elements of Islamic culture – referred to as "culture of the mind", "qualities", "science", "morals" (literally) and "the best form of all affairs" in major references – all belong to a high concept: wisdom and philosophy.

This wisdom includes any kind of activity able to enhance objective lifestyles for each individual or society. The first founder and promoter of this culture is God, who granted man the means to write, talent, the power to express himself, taste, and the constant desire for seeking perfection and stable basics in the ever-flowing stream of events.

As a result of this culture:

" Three centuries after the Holy Prophet died, the city of Qartaba, with a population of one million, had eighty academic schools and a library including 600,000 books; Arabic had become the main language of science. During this era, knowledge resumed spreading around the world.

Zachariah Razi (251-313HQ) did a thorough study on smallpox, and his colleague Abul-qassem Khalaf bin-Abbass Zahravi (d. 404HQ) did the same for wen and spinal bone diseases.

Avicenna (370-428HQ), named "the prince of science", had upgraded medicine in the Islamic society to such an extent that when one of the kings of Castill caught smallpox, he asked his enemies in Qartaba for help.

Mohammad ibn-Jaber-ibn Senan Battani (d.317) has brought much honor to his country through his famous works. A noble aristocrat, Battani had great respect for Ptolemy, although he himself exceeded Ptolemy in accurately studying the equinox

---

[1]- See Appendix .

calendar, and was the first to use the sinus instead of the hypothenus, which led to today's trigonometry."[1]

Literary culture as a whole – the voice of any cultural ideal – became such a mighty creative factor in Islamic societies that by presenting Jala-il-din Mowlavi and his like, it influenced all other constructive cultures around the world, and any literary school of thought today recognizes Mowlavi as one of its constituents.

However, other ordinary cultures do not enjoy such systematic establishment.

Let us take the statement "Literary and artistic modernity inhibits scientific advances"[2] into more careful consideration. By comparing it with the article "Scientific Bankruptcy Announced"[3], what may we conclude ...?!

On the other hand, had the need for organizing and saturating all of man's psychic aspects been taken into consideration while constructing and continuing cultural changes, certainly no advance in one cultural affect would inhibit the others; in other words, literary and artistic modernism would not prevent science from developing,and inappropriate expectations of observation, experience, or ignorance towards ideological culture and scientific bankruptcy would never happen.

As we have already stated:

"The culture established by Islam is an aimed life that strongly activates human aspects of aesthetism, desire for knowledge, logic, and idealism, and organizes all cultural elements."

Artistic constructions in Spain, India, Iran and Syria – about the highly exquisite qualities of which all scholars on art agree – depict how strongly Islam enhances aesthetic aspects.

The Koran has pointed out God-made beauty on seven occasions, for instance:

"We have adorned the lower heaven with the adornment of the stars".[4]

1- Jean-Pierre Rosseau, *The History of Science*.
2- Ibid.
3- Ibid.
4- The Rangers (37): 6.

"We have set in heaven constellations, adorned them out to beholders."[1]

"Say: Who has forbidden the ornament of God which he brought forth for His servants, and the good things of his providing?"[2]

In the above verses, "ornament" and "adorning" refer to beauty, both in its general and special meanings. The first two verses show its special meaning, and the third refers generally to any attractive, useful phenomenon.

The plentiful Koranic verses encouraging thought had such a profound mental effect on Muslims that very soon Islam became the focal point of science and knowledge. During the dark Medieval era, when all countries were deprived of any knowledge, Muslims successfully kept the flame of science burning. Other cultural elements, such as moral ethics and idealism, also highly flourished. All of these organized advances were due to their being based on the original principle of the objectiveness of life. If the basis is destroyed, all effects arising in the name of culture will also be of compulsory origin, showing fake liveliness like a water-sprinkled flower cut from its stem.

Can a Society Have Various Cultures?

Before we answer this question, we must determine what is meant by "various" cultures. Let us consider some different kinds of culture:

First: cultures able to coexist in harmony due to their original commonalities, e.g. the cultures of holy religions (Islam, the Jews, Christianity, Zoroastrianism, and any other religion able to verify its holy origin).

The best reason for the potential for harmony among the above-mentioned cultures is the vast amount of various vital qualities that have made all divine religions ever since Abraham (s.a.w.), uniting people from many religious bases.

We clearly see how Islam, by providing freedom of belief and culture for the religiously intellectual, made harmony possible between them and Muslims, and all were able to

---

1- The El-Hijr (15): 16.
2- The Battlements (7):32.

endeavor in fields of science, ideology, industry, and culture throughout various eras of history; it seems the Islamic civilization has belonged to them all.

Can history ever deny the intimate, sincere co-operations various religions have made in medicine, in hospitals and research centers around the world since many years ago?[1]

The real commonalities between various religions causing their harmony are original realities such as: 1. The source of the universe (God); 2. God's wisdom and will in order to emancipate and perfect man (by giving them logical thought, conscience, and great prophets); 3. the realness of eternity; 4. the fact that God Almighty is truly the greatest and wisest; 5. all divine religions agree on the fact that man deserves a meritorious life, and is definitely entitled to dignity, graciousness, chastity, responsible freedom, education in all spiritual and/or physical matters.

Of course, all religions agree on the basic rights in Abraham's religion; therefore, they should also be in agreement on any cultural element based on these rights.

Second: cultures harmoniously common in fundamental ideologies and basics of natural life, and also cultures having the same ideas about the optimum, logical life – though their common points may not be religious.

Examples are celebrations after victory over a common enemy threatening all people's lives; also, commonalities in creating arts that depict man-made advances towards a better life in this world.

Third: cultures that conflict in their ideas and concepts of the universe, particularly in their interpretation of life and its primary end.

Even if such cultures do not neutralize each other, obviously their differences would in time make them all "colorless" cultures in coexistence; however, since their "colorlessness" is due to disturbing conflicts, they would never be capable of harmony.

There are numerous examples of these cultures, like the contrast between Iran's national culture and its religious

---

1- Especially during late 2nd to late 5th centuries Hijra.

culture – Islam. Of course, their "contrast" does not imply that they cannot harmoniously coexist; contrarily, as we see, the elements of national culture – based on the real issues of physical and spiritual life – that can play a useful role to mentally prepare people to accept factors leading to prosperity, are also accepted in the religious culture, like artistic poetry which is a highly popular art in Iran. Provided being applied in accordance with facts serving man's prosperity, this cultural element is not only undoubtedly accepted by Islam, but even strongly encouraged by some religious references to be used to develop descriptions of realities about the world and man as they should be.

The criterion for cultural harmony lies in those affairs useful for man's physical and spiritual life. Such high cooperation and harmony between national and religious cultures caused Iranians to begin the greatest of scientific, philosophical, artistic, industrial, legal and moral services in the framework of Islamic culture, thus raising Iran to its pinnacle of flourish. Let us now briefly address national, religious and western cultures and their compatibility with Iranian culture.

Those who claim Iran is capable of having three different cultures, should first consider the fact that, when added to a land, "nation" is not just a word anymore; Iran's history goes way back in time, and our country has seen various cultures in different eras. These scholars should be asked, therefore, which one of Iran's culture they mean.

Iranian culture has gone through various periods; the Arian invasion; the Medes era; the Achmanid era; the Arsacides; the Parthians; the Keyan dynasty; the Sasanids; and many other ears after the rise of Islam. Are the commonalities among all of these eras meant here?[1]

Is Islamic Culture Compatible with Western Culture?

---

[1]- For further study on the differences among various cultural eras in the history of Iran, see Hassan Pirnia, The Ancient History of Iran, ⇨ Vol; and also Will Durant, *The History of Civilization*, Vol. 1 (The East, the Cradle of Civilization).

If by "culture" here we refer to phenomena making man's intelligible life understanding, objective and mentally enlighting, it is not only certainly compatible with Islamic culture, but also even encouraged and promoted by it. The criterion is, however, whether Western culture is capable of basing itself upon an objective man in an objective world or not.

During the last decade of the twentieth century, hedonism and utilitarianism dominated man's life goals in the West. Of course, we do not mean to deny the unquestionable figures and goodwill intentions occurring in Western countries. But the dominant trends are, as we mentioned above, mixed with various forms of opportunist authoritarianism.

In brief, Islamic culture is based upon a "intelligible life", which originates from the commonalities among divine religions (actually, all from Abraham's religion); undoubtedly, any culture – Western or Eastern – able to adjust itself to these common basics can have a profound role alongside Islamic cultures in reviving the prosperity of human societies.

Therefore, those who opinionate on the possibility of three harmonious cultures (national, religious and Western) coexisting in Iran, are either not thoroughly aware about them, or have been lured to express such ideas.

Now let us consider the basics of today's culture in the West, and see whether they are acceptable in Islamic culture or not.

First, we should keep in mind that the fundamentals of Western culture do not account for all of its people's thoughts and interest – the definitions given in dictionaries and encyclopedias verify this, too – and are merely facts consisting the foundation of their culture, or maybe imposed by authoritative force.

Therefore, persons or phenomena exist in their life-styles which contradict the basics of their culture. Some of the fundamentals of contemporaryWestern culture are:

1. Worldly life: man's "last" stop. Stated in most Western works, it makes up for the majority of Western scientific culture. Unfortunately, the authoritative power of science – sometimes even more forceful and inhuman than Medieval infidelity – is at times used for verifying this basic of their culture; scientific

appearance, obviously, is sometimes much more harmful than scientific outcomes.

Thus, with all of the evidence given by human conscience and pure logic that the world cannot be the end of man, relying on science in order to deny this fact will not only make science seem worthless, but even stupifying.

2. Absolute freedom for any individual or group, provided that they do not disturb others' legal rights Thus, individuals must have no legal confinement in life at all; one can commit the filthiest of actions, and nobody can stop him/her.

Let us remind those who "expertly" tend to mix Western culture with Islamic culture about quotations made by the US Attorney of State:

> "For an American, law and religion cannot conflict more. Western countries, even those that do not insist on the boundary between religion and politics, consider the law as just a worldly issue highly influenced by current affairs ... which legislators and law courts are to carry out. The government should control it totally, not churches or religion. Thus, the law we have in America cleverly by-passes religion, and only breezes past moral dutifulness. In other words, an American can be law-abiding and still morally deteriorated."[1]

Can a culture only considering man's coexistence and legal rights towards other people ever be compatible with a culture that takes account of all human aspects, guiding them in a law-supported "logical" path?

3. The essence of power: although the essence of power is generally not a main component of Western culture – it is even still rejected in some Western literary and more works – but alas, its influence shows in every aspect of today's political and social culture in the West – particularly the practical aspects. Even cooperation, teamwork, appreciation for one's peers and their decisions is considered a device for achieving power; thus, the current trend in Western culture is not "Death is the natural destination for the weak; no powerful dies before weakening", but the strong trying hard to weaken people in their own

---

- Herbert J. Lisbani, *Law in Islam*.1

physical aspects, leaving them to struggle towards their "natural destination": death!

4. The essence of pleasure: Not only does Western culture encourage pleasure in life, it even uses scientific jargon to justify it: "Depriving oneself of pleasures leads to complexes and other psychological abnormalities!"

Although these passionate lovers of fame admit that leaving pleasures causes mental activities to weaken:

> *Nihil est religio et precatio ejus nisi penis: his thought has borne him down to the lowest depth. [His religion and his prayer (is) nothing but the penis: his thought has borne him down to the lowest depth]*

(Rumi, Masnavi, Book 2: 3151)

They did not expand the concept to the pleasures of science, mystic knowledge, helping others, justice and piety.

5. The essence of profit-making and opportunism: Utilitarianism is so obviously established in the West that there seems no need to prove its dominance through reasoning, explanations and surveys. This part of Western culture claims man to be constantly seeking his own benefits: "No one can stop me from achieving what is to my advantage; I am entitled to take as my own anything I consider advantageous to me, even though it may harm others." Is this correct, or had we not better say, "Nobody has the right to harm or damage what I have?"

From logical, moral, legal, philosophical and religious points of view, definitely the latter is correct. It is totally immoral to let people appropriate anything they consider to their advantage! This can be claimed only when all people have the right to deflect harm coming to them.

6. Machiavellian trends in political culture: This method weakens all human rules and principles to the benefit of politicians' goals – who are definitely unaware of man's various needs – thus making everything unimportant in their viewpoint.

It is true to state that ever since Machiavellian methods stepped into human management, the essence and formality of mankind has suffered irrevocably. We shall address another point on this matter in the next item.

7. Spreading pragmatism without correctly interpreting it: If it were interpreted so that it claimed abstract, unreal concepts useless and inapplicable for find out the truth about the universe – since they are neither receivable nor practically usable – we could regard it as logical and acceptable, but the actual case is, the only criterion used to judge issues is clearly observable, outer actions. However, man's critical mental, spiritual and physical needs cannot be considered as acts; hope, goodwill, recognition of observable, logical beauty, justice and spiritual persistence and dutifulness are highly superior to utilitarianism, and are the highest ideals and pillars of morality of most great religions', for they pertain to man's spiritual grandeur.

When a culture considers the observable actions as the criterion, it has in fact ignored the most fundamentally important element of evolution: man's spiritual development.

8. Limiting scientific knowledge: Limiting knowledge to what can be observed merely by physical senses and human-made laboratories, confines the primary factor in man's development – religion, morals , wisdom, mystic knowledge and other originally mental realities of man's soul, the omission of which led to 'The Bankruptcy of Science", and human survival in the 21st century was put into great danger.[1]

9. Presenting irrelevant issues in the name of philosophy and ideology: It is an undeniable fact that for many years, not only has the West failed to come up with an organized, systematic philosophical ideology, but even ignored the need to define some deeply meaningful concepts. Man, on the other hand cannot freely interpret and explain life without understanding the general basics of the four connections (man-himself, man-God, man-the universe, and man-other people).

10. Prosaic arts: It is quite surprising how "arts" can be combined with the "prosaic", which refers to anything low and destroying high human morals. The prosaic, referring to all of the immoral, cannot exist alongside art, which arises out of perfection.

1- Mohammad Taghi Jafari, *The Message of Mind,* from the lecture   *"Survival in the 21st Century"*, UNESCO Symposium on 21st Century   Culture and Science, Vancouver, Canada, September 1989.

Today's Western art – if it can be called art – merely aims to astonish its viewers. The more amazed they become, the more artistic a work can be considered! On the other hand, any prosy, root-drying, meaningless phenomenon can be presented to the unaware in a highly attractive form, and still cause the same amount of amazement. But can such spectacles reveal any of the realities concerning man's objective path of life? What kind of persons will the outcomes of these kinds of art be? Neither these arts, not their creators, have been able to answer such questions so far.

As a whole, cultural triteness and employing culture to serve physical desires, utilitarianism and auth-oritarianism, is enough to destroy any culture, for when man falls into banality and unlimited physical desires, he has no identity left to provide a culture with.

Moral Corruption is the Main Reason for the Deterioration of Western Culture

Let us now quote from Mr. Robert G. Ringer's statements, which are of the most alerting cries of the human soul in Western societies – drowning in mechanized infidelity, insensibility due to superficial, limited desires – depicting the fall of original, human cultures:

"What has caused the conditions of life in the West to change so much? Why have all of the good qualities vanished?

In my opinion, the answer lies in the cleverly-laid conditions of 'Abiding by Gradually-Imposed Principles'. A highly effective technique, abiding by gradually-imposed principles becomes even stronger when man has some dependencies. Let us go into greater detail. Studies have shown that man does not respond positively to sudden changes; in fact, he goes into defense and puts up a strong resistance. However, there is also much evidence that shows man cannot resist gradual changes, a fact well-understood by the enemies of individual liberty. They are clever enough to realize that they must act patiently. History clearly shows than that the world cannot be changed in two weeks. However, by moving step by step towards their goals, no one would ever notice their evil plans infiltrate people's lives. Thus, people give in to *gradual changes*, considering it their destiny.

Some generations may consider a particular lifestyle as slavery, whereas other generations may think of it as freedom, for each generation knows only its own lifestyle. Thus, the deterioration of Western societies is the strongest evidence for the influence of these gradually imposing methods.

People have grown accustomed to the crisis around them; they have accepted the decadence, corruption and chaos that fills their surroundings. Only hope keeps them going; all they think of is when the demise may happen. Few people, however, believe it would ever take place, for such falls are mostly based on momentary actions. The demise of the West fills quite a fluctuating diagram. America has deteriorated much faster during the years 1913 to 1963 than the previous 137 years. Among those fifty years, the last two decades prove to be more intense. However, there is no concrete evidence that deterioration accelerates every year, or that the Western civilization is nearing its demise; but it is definite that the present condi-tions will not be able to carry on easily. Although man has always faced problems, we now have many more problems than our predecessors, anyone over thirty years of age – by just looking carefully around him – will definitely agree on this. Unfortunately, however, most people do not even want to realize the danger threatening them. Their way of reasoning is quite amazing. They believe that if one neglects the problems and dangers ('Whatever will be, will be'), everything will look normal to him; his worries will fade away."[1]

Mr. Ringer thus accounts for the rise of human rights at the time morals are disappearing in the West:

"When all moral ethics in the West were about to fall, Human Rights arose like a sacred belief – or, better said, a major law (or right) – and gradually turned into a strong bond of unity among people. Whatever we name it – republic, mass, population,... is irrelevant! In a democracy, human rights means safeguarding the borders of the country, which is the best way to satisfy the people. But the crucially important point is, many consider it in its

---

1- Robert G. Ringer, *The Fall of Western Civilization.*

lowest meaning: violating others' rights in the name of the 'majority's rights'; in other words, the stronger is always right! Such concepts are obviously in no way compatible with justice or morality."[1]

When asked, "Is it too late?" Mr. Ringer says:

"I am frequently asked whether it is too late to save Western civilization or not. I believe the question is incomplete. Keep in mind that moral revolution has come to an end, for those social laws giving the rights and authority to desires – based on the idea that 'Man is Entitled to His Desires', thus making chaos a sacred law – have reached their peak. So the more appropriate question will be: Can we rediscover and recover our former moral qualities? Can we ever make those moral values again the base of our civilization?

If we can, there should be no worry whether it may be too late; there is no reason to believe we are incapable of providing people in the West with a new life. In my opinion, the only hope is to rediscover Western civilization by means of correct moral values. Therefore, we should be brave, wise, and consciously try to find what destroyed these moral values, and then rebuild them."[2]

Mr. Ringer should keep only one thing in mind: If he used "human civilization" instead of "Western civilization", both the East and the West could be saved; ignoring the East and solely focusing on the West would prove aimless, for the two are strongly related. Is only considering the West not racist favoritism?

This, indeed, is the destructive factor, which originates from selfishness, and is the root of all problems in our times – especially in the West.

Now let us consider the views of the renowned scholar, Erich Fromm, on the effect of cultural deterioration on the humanities in particular:

- *"Man is the only being that kills its kind without any biological reason.*
- *Modern psychology is quite lifeless, for it easily cuts a human into different parts, ignoring a whole, living human being. In other words, it considers man as a set of certain*

- Ibid.1
- Ibid.2

qualities put together – like a machine – and totally overlooks him as being alive.

- *Nowadays, man is considered as a tool still without a machine to be used in. A complete human sees himself/herself as an active piece of goods (in other words, an independent item of merchandise); hence, he is lonely and miserable. However, he tries to save himself from his misery. He is searching for happiness, but is fighting a losing battle.*

- *In today's societies, man has become a zero, a part of a machine; as long as a society sees profit-making and production as man's highest end, this is inevitable. I believe today's social establishment has destructive roots, for it produces tendencies for destruction. The greater the tendency for destruction, the more miserable man will be, and in turn less positive towards life."*[1]

Factors Stabilizing Cultures throughout History

Some cultures or cultural elements certainly seem more stable than others. Various theories have been proposed accounting for their stability, and it is quite useful to study them. First, we should keep in mind that some cultures have not at all remained firm due to their elements being general human virtual facts – in fact, they should be regarded as man's virtual elements "as they are."

Studying these cultures may make their scholars and followers put serious effort into finding the natural reason brought about by their geographical, economic, social, political and historic aspect; thus, through realistic assessment of their cultures, they may refine and advance human ideals and come to dynamic, objective cultures.

For instance, slavery was a culture that even great scholars like Aristotle approved of; although it covered all human qualities in its own framework of slavery, it was still a totally incorrect culture that dominated most ancient lands. However, this culture cunningly rules out one of the most vital virtues of man – responsible freedom – thus upsetting man's developed thoughts into a state of confusion and disorder. Islam, on the

---

other hand, considered slavery a phenomenon totally irrelevant to man's "actual" virtues, and set out to demolish it.

Thus, the reason for the stability and deep influence of a culture cannot abstractly lie in its human virtual reality. In order to recognize if a culture is truly useful and stable, therefore, we need not the period of time of its duration, but its basic factors. A few of the basic factors that stabilize cultures are:

Factor One: the positive relationship between a culture – or some of its components – and the needs or luxuries of the members of a society. For example, the unique culture concerning living beings in India is based on regional factors or beliefs about living this only see in that area; likewise, the traditions of Norooz (the new year celebrations) in Iran are due to Iran's climate, and have been established for many years.

Factor Two: is time; the more aged cultural elements become, the higher their value will be. It is impossible to account for this factor, but we can say that firmness during a long time can be sign of stability in cultural elements; however, it is not enough to prove it.

Selfishness has existed throughout the whole history of mankind; very few cases can be found in which man has succeeded in keeping his virtues aligned with true logic and used them correctly – the majority have fallen astray in assessing "themselves", and instead of having the proper "self" (safeguarding their innate virtues up to perfection), they fall into ill-mannered selfishness. Such examples bring us to the conclusion that the stability of a culture in human lives does not necessarily imply its righteousness, although anything advantageous to man can prove original, and will remain firm for a long time.

Factor Three: the formation of the culture of traditions, customs and beliefs plays a crucial role in giving a society a special nationality, and causes the people to be focused and organized. Soon these cultural elements will turn into the identity of the society, which it will defend to the last breath; of course, this is due to the fact that as time goes by, there is more communication among cultures, which in turn enhances cultural studies and research, and modifications would prove necessary.

Factor Four: the compatibility of cultures with facts and realities is verifiable. The stronger and deeper their compatibility, the better the stability of the cultural elements.

Apart from the second factor – which considers cultural stability as due to time and duration – the other above-mentioned factors do not do so. In case of the first factor, the reasons and necessities leading to the beliefs of the society require concern. If they are based on the psychological rules of the peoples, time will undoubtedly be unable to influence it. And if it depends on the personal beliefs of the intellectual figures in the society, two factors will determine its survival:

a. the qualitative and quantitative influence of the outstanding figures in the society;

b. their qualitative and quantitative background logically supporting their culture's stability.

If the supporting factor is their cultural crystallization – directing the people as a truly original establishment – the culture will be deeply engraved in people's souls, and can strongly unite them. This is why time will not be able to influence it, for it enjoys logical backing.[1]

1- We read in ancient Egyptian law books – dating 3000 years back in   time – that the first thing the accused should be asked is, "Does your   conscience approve of what you tell the judge?" Such agreement bet-   ween conscience

Blind Imitation of Past Beliefs and Cultures Inhibits Logical Thought and Wisdom

We have already accepted that the firm establishment of culture among people does not necessarily imply that it enjoys originality or is compatible with reality. Although a culture well-engraved in people's lives and souls does become a viewpoint to man and the world, many cultures past and present lose all of their composure when it comes to logical analysis, therefore man must analysis the dominant culture of his society and eliminate any sedimentary, baseless elements in it if he wants to take positive steps towards "elevating evolutionary life." But alas, sometimes imitation dominates great minds so much that all of man's thoughts are blocked. It seems we deny the fact that:

Imitation destroyed people; a thousand damns be upon imitation!
(Mowlavi)

How can an imitator also be a researcher? How can a wise one be the same as a fool?

Centuries come and go, but society leaders still do not understand how destructively inhibiting imitation is. Maybe they are afraid that without imitation in people's individual and social life, they would not need management anymore … have they not ever thought that the power-greedy must first change from "person" to "thing" – in other words, from "researcher" to "imitator" – before they can change people, take advantage of them, and imprison them in a cage of illogical imitation?

In brief, depriving people of sin, recognizing true life and its rules is a greatly unforgivable and deserves no less than being banned from God's kind blessings.

Blindly following the beliefs and traditions of the predecessors ruins one's mind; likewise following those drowning in their animal desires, those who have totally put aside human morals or dignity in the name of freedom,

---

and speech in ancient Egyptian legal culture can still   be regarded as a solemn truth.

modernity, progress, culture and so on, using such deceiving jargon to destroy all logic, consciousness or conscience. This is not an Eastern theory or religious prejudice, for we can see even more intense reflections of such hatred for Western leaders by Western scholars themselves; in an interview with *Spiegel*, one of them has said, "Shame is fading away, and the urge to kill no longer knows any bounds. The mass media – television and radio stations the most – have brazenly begun to use force and impudence in order to attract more customers for the general industry. Cultural critics are complaining about inadvertent violence, and have announced a moral disaster condition. Sociologists, psychologists and politicians are angry with the sexual corruption presented in all cultural areas – TV and the film industry in particular. The confusion caused by insolence and violation is so great that even the Liberal Church of the Bible cries out about it in its publications.

"The women in Bayer have signed petitions demanding laws against sexual misconduct and violence. Sociologists discuss subjects like 'violence in arts' or 'tendencies towards new terror'. The *Frankfurter Alegmaina Zeitung* has spoken of unprecedentedly high violence in the community, claiming a state of moral disaster which has engulfed the whole urban areas. As violence and harassment changes from a forbidden crime to a hobby, unprotected, confused humanity tries to condemn the increasing pressure and oppression upon foreigners, violence in streets, stadiums and public transport vehicles.

Freud's mysterious statement comes to mind:
"The lack of shame is a sign of mental weakness. The conscience does not function anymore."

Spiegel: Mr. Duerr[1], violence and violations are increasing day by day. What is wrong with this society?

Duerr: In my opinion, the basic problem is the destruction of social relationships, which leads to what man calls emotional death – in other words, the "end of warmth."

1- From an interview with German anthropologist Hans Peter Duerr, in the *Spiegel*, No. 2, 1993.

The mass media also accelerate it by spreading it so much. Although our modern, free society has brought us happiness, there is one problem with this freedom – it took away from us the warmth that used to exist among families, and dominated man's social conduct.

Spiegel: How is the demise of family attachment related to the lack of shame?

Duerr: They are definitely related. For instance, physical shame means limiting the signs of sexual behavior in order to keep a personal relationship chaste.

Nowadays, people have no respect for selected friendships. Therefore, privatizing sexual attraction is meaningless.

Spiegel: What if brazenness grows? If physical shame – as you have stated – arises from man's nature – how can we witness impudence increase every day?

Duerr: The Pope and the high priests are still in deep discussion on the nature of man. Sociologists, on the other hand, also stubbornly resist. What I'm trying to say is that, however people's social life may have formed, physical shame plays a critical role in it, for it can reduce social frustrations, and strengthen the relationships between married couples; that is why with shame fading away, adultery has increased to such an extent.

Spiegel: But this freedom is highly publicized, contrary to your theory.

Duerr: There certainly has been no society yet in which personal relationships are really so intensly publicized. This behavior has also led to violence. It seems to be unprecedented throughout history.

Spiegel: Freud spoke of a lack of shame that weakens the wisdom of mind.

Duerr: That is true; there comes a time when man realizes that his own incompetence has led to a great lack of culture and civilization. Progress-orientated theorists have always claimed that primitive societies enjoyed much more zeal, endeavor, desire and uncontrollable instincts that we do in our well-established society today."1

It is needless to mention how strongly Islamic culture and other divine religions have repeatedly warned man about the role of lust and undisciplined life in weakening thoughts.

"Nihil est religio et precatio ejus nisi penis: his thought has borne him down to the lowest depth. [His religion and his prayer (is) nothing but the penis: his thought has borne him down to the lowest depth.]
Though he rise to the sky, be not afraid of him, for (it is only) in love of lowness (degradation) he has studied (and gained eminence).
He gallops his horse towards lowness, albeit he rings the bell (proclaims that he is going) aloft.
What is there to fear from the flags of beggars? — for those flags are (but) a means for (getting) a mouthful of bread.
(Rumi, Masnavi, Book 2: 3151-3154).
Faith, the highest outcome of logical thought and elevated emotions, is destroyed by shamelessness.

Imam Ali (A.S.) has said:
"One who has no shame, has no faith."
Although Freud states that, "The lack of shame is a sign of mental weakness", how can he – with all of his emphasis on the necessity of saturating sexual instincts in any way possible – consider the lack of shame as a sign of a weak mind?

Culture Adoption (Acculturation) and Its Causes

Cultural adoption has become quite popular these days. As religion-opposed, immoral activities and phenomena are infiltrating religious societies2, the nobly dignified ones become more and more terrified.

We shall address culture adoption by considering a few points:

1- These theorists do not prefer "unlimited" lifestyles in order to enjoy civilized excitement or desire, for civilized people act on their   elevated spiritual talents; thus, bringing instincts under control – in   particular insatiable hedonism, which is the strongest – is of crutial   necessity.
2- We do not mean completely religious or highly moral societies, but   those not yet engulfed by immorals and lack of religion.

One: From an absolute point of view, is culture adoption wrong or right? What is included in the cultural concepts and elements being accepted?

Obviously, the third part of this question is correct, and it must be determined what kind of culture is being accepted. If it is "the suitable methods or meritorious qualities for those of man's physical or mental activities based on logical reasoning in sensible life", such a culture would undoubtedly be accepted, as it has been throughout history – man's perfectionist potential would seek it under any circumstances.

The most evident example possible for this is the Muslims' fantastic endeavors throughout the 2nd through 5th centuries (Hijra) which innately aimed to establish culture, civilization and adopt the meritorious, suitable aspects from other countries. From the Caspian shores to the Atlantic waters, they prevented their original, evolutional culture from demise. Such pioneers of culture and civilization indeed discarded any filthy, immoral phenomena that opposed religion in the name of culture, and only considered those realities which were advantageous to man's physical and spiritual life as culture.

Two: Adopting dynamic, objective (evolutionary) cultures, although quite vital, does not mean imitation without studying, examining and refining.

Imitation ruined people; a thousand damns be upon imitation!

(Mowlavi)

Imitation is destructively wrong, no matter whether something good or bad is imitated; in any case, the copycat is totally unaware of what he is doing. The only difference is, if a meritorious reality is being imitated, it will lead to good effects, despite without the role of the imitator. Literary culture quite clearly elaborates on this:

One who calls God is much different from one who knows God; as different as men are from animals.

Thus, the God-knowers to God-seekers are like mystic knowledge to science.

The shining sun is not the same as the shining moon; each shining differs from the other.

How can a researcher be considered equal to a copycat? How can the knowing be the same as the ignorant?[1]

If only the laws forbidding copying were seriously followed, there would be no more fluctuation in scientific theories, philosophy and other cultural elements. Recently, "scientific" theories have infiltrated Islamic societies from the West, and have been imitatively accepted by the unaware as scientific discoveries. If they were told that such issues lack a soundly scientific basis and are merely subjective deductions or assumptions, they would abruptly disagree, "No! You are decadent! You are opposing science! The time for using imagination has come to an end.

This is science, the only thing that can bring about our progress. "These ignorant – and, at times spiteful – people forced others to follow such theories, abusing universally accepted principles like "Scientific rules cannot be disagreed with." Since their obedience was merely imitation, even when the theories were scientifically proved wrong and rejected in the West, the copycats insisted on their beliefs – as if the clear blue sky were still pouring rain on their houses![2]

1- The second verses is from Allameh Jafari and rest are from Frooghi Bastami.

2- For instance, a) when the essence of sexual instincts and their priority over all other aspects had become popular in the past, some people in the East presented it as a scientific rule. After a while, a few psychologists like Adler and Jung discarded the theory. The writer has even heard from the late scholar Dr. Mirsepasi – who was a close friend of Freud – that his theory was more like a force, rather than a scientific issue. Later, some psychological experts claimed that the essence of safeguarding one's virtues and personality was the deepest, most active of the instincts, and took Freud's theory under more intense criticism.

However, some of our academic institutions still consider it a scientific issue! Such mental deviation is a result of copying scientific culture, which destroys all truth-seeking spirits in man. b) As we all know, the theory of animal evolution to higher species was proposed by Lamarke and Darwin in the 19th century. Their accounts were no more than a novel theory. However, it infiltrated our society like a scientific law of concrete proof. But as time went by and more research was made, it was shown to lack evidence, and soon fell into dark obscurredness.

Three: There are various forms of culture transferring to other societies. Let us now study:

Culture Transfer

1. Culture transfer is best in its useful, productive form, which includes realities concerning meritorious methods for man's "intelligible life." Such cultural elements – like science, industries, religious qualities and elements based only upon man's pure virtues – are not only suitable enough for everyone to cooperate in their transfer, but also Islam has considered it a religious duty.

Many Islamic references have emphasized on such cooperation. The Holy Koran says:

"Help one another to piety and good fearing; do not help each other to sin and enmity. There is no piety or good deed in this world higher than spreading elevating cultures that can save man from ignorance, poverty, anxiety, and various needs. And fear God, for surely he is terrible in retribution."[1]

The Holy Prophet has also said:

All people are related to God; those who are more useful for others, are the most favored by God.

There remains no doubt that only life-saving cultures are the most vital and the most advantageous to man.

In all major references on history and civilization – written whether by Western or Eastern researchers – it is agreed that when Muslims were free of their selfish, tyrant rules during the 3rd through 5th centuries (Hijra), they had the chance to adopt cultural elements from other nations of that time, expand their culture and civilization, and pass on their own useful cultural elements alongside the elements adopted, adjusted and refined; some historians have stated this era as being crucial to the protection of science and culture in the Medieval times.

In his seminal Biographical Encyclopedia of Science and Technology (1972), Isaac Asimov has stated:

For further study, please see Pierre Rosseau, *The History of Industry and Inventions.*

1- The Table (5). 2.

"The Arabs occupied Syria in the 630s and Egypt in the 640s. In so doing, they fell heir to much of Greek science, and this proved of importance and even benefit to the history of science and even to the survival of civilized world from the onslaughts of barbers.

During the whole era of the Eastern Roman Empire, science had no opportunity to flourish, since there was no scientific circle around to sustain the ideas. For a thousand years of Byzantine history, the only name worth mentioning is Callinicus. Western Europe was in darkness. It was the Arabs alone who were in a position to preserve and transit human scientific heritage. Not only through the translation of Greek scientific and philosophical works did Arabs help human knowledge to survive, but they also produced some brilliant works in certain fields of science and enriched the scientific heritage. Alchemy was one of the branches of science that was taken seriously by Muslims and built into great heights."

Geoge Sarton has also appreciated Muslims' contribution in the following words:

Perhaps the main, as well as the least obvious, achievement of the middle ages was the creation of the experimental spirit, or more exactly, its slow incubation. This was primarily due to Muslims down to the end of the twelfth century, then to the Christians.

He continues his appraisal as follows:

The briefest enumeration of the Arabic [Islamic] contributions to knowledge would be too long to be inserted here, but I must insist on the fact that, though a major part of the activity of Arabic-writing scholars consisted in the translation of Greek works and their assimilation, they in fact did far more than that. They did not simply transmit ancient knowledge, they created a new one. To be sure, none of them attained the highest peaks of the Greek genius. No Arabic mathematician can begin to compare with Archimedes or Apollonius. Avicenna makes one think of Galen, but no Arabic physician had the wisdom of Hippocrates. However, such comparisons are hardly fair, for a few Greeks had reached, almost suddenly, extraordinary heights. That is what we call the Greek miracle. But one might speak also, though in a different sense, of an Arabic [i.e., Islamic] miracle. The creation of a new civilization of international and encyclopedic magnitude within less than two centuries is something that we can describe, but not completely explain.

Moreover, Philipp Frank has openly written:

In the middle ages no nation has as much contributed to the progress and advance of humanity as the Muslims did.

In her renowned "Allahs Sonne über dem Abendland" ("Allah's Sun over the Occident") (1960), Sigrid Hunke states:

We are not only an heir to Greece and Roma, but we are indeed the inheritor of Islamic intellectual world which the Occident is undoubtedly indebted to.

Gustav Le Bon's La Civilization de Islam et Arab is quite informing in this regard. This French sociologist has honestly written:

Islam treated humen beings living in the lands conquered by Muslims with fairness and affection and in accordance with the basic principles of humanity.

The agents of Islamic administration were so unflinching in their pact and treated the people so graciously that they chose Islam and Arabic with open arms. I should reiterate again that such achievements cannot be ever obtained by the force of the sword, and the conquerors who have entered Egypt never could have scored such successes.

Bertrand Russell confesses that:

In scientific discoveries – particularly in chemistry – Muslims were more experimental than the Greeks. They sought to transmute the metals into gold, to uncover the mystery of alchemy and to acquire the elixir of life. These were indeed their chief motives to devote themselves to chemistry, Russell argues.

Throughout the dark ages of the Christian world, it was in fact Muslims, according to Russell, who sustained human civilization and those scientific ideas, which were later developed by such medieval thinkers, as Roger Bacon was mainly drawn on Muslim intellectual heritage.

2. Transferring useful cultural elements, in order to gain economic or political advantages. In other words, the society intends to spread useful cultural elements to other societies in order to profit economically politically, or even dominate them; the purpose is not to follow ideal human goals or expanding helpful cultures. In these cases, the communities or nations conceding the cultures must take into careful consideration what they are adopting; otherwise, they would end up with a load of nonsense called "culture", which would eventually ruin them.

As the renowned Iranian poet Nezami Ganjavi writes:

"What are they endeavoring for?" one asked." He was told,
"They buy sorrow at the expense their lives.

3. Transferring culture in order to present the society as a leading pioneer to other societies.

Although such meagre intention may seem unimportant at first, they can lead to destructive aftermaths, for they all originate from selfishness; furthermore, they may even humiliate the society receiving their culture, and demand a reward for elevating their culture: "Indeed, our brain tissue is quite different from yours; we are much more complete, and as you know, the principle of evolution states that the superior can consider themselves as the goal, and others the means to achieve it!"

4. Transferring spiritually or physically corruptive and harmful factors to others in the name of culture may possibly be the most vexed of human actions towards their peers. Since "intelligible culture" is the key element of an intelligible life, then one can feasibly argue that anti-cultural phenomena are key to human spiritual demise. Creating and presenting sexually arousing devices on a large scale – though seemingly scientifically-based phenomena or depicting beauty – actually aims to destroy mankind.

5. The production of stories, paintings or other forms of "art" implying nihilistic goals, however exquisite they may be, is equal to destroying human beings.

6. Creating any works of art – no matter how attractive or fascinating – that humiliates and ridicules human character is equal to murder.

7. Efforts towards establishing ignorance about social problems and neglecting the poor; cultural effects clearly show this.

8. Any efforts towards depriving people of their responsible freedom, grace, dignity and the life they deserve is equivalent to destroying their souls, no matter what or how the cultural activities may be.

9.   Any seemingly-cultural efforts towards distracting human beings from eternity and the origin and end of life, is not different from trying to annihilate man's goal – seeking spirit.

Now we indeed realize what a massacre goes on among human communities, or as Gibran Khalil Gibran puts it, "Not only are the murderers of human souls ignorantly enjoying themselves, but they are even publicly announced guilty of murder, and still the 'dead' souls around them do not touch them."

> *"The justice there is now on earth brings demons to tears, and makes the dead laugh at its sight."*
>
> *"Prisons and death is for the smaller, weaker criminals; the strong criminals enjoy glory and honor."*
>
> *"If one steals a flower, he is condemned and humiliated; if one steals the whole field, he is considered a significant hero." 1*
>
> *"Murderers of bodies are punished, but killers of human spirits walk about feely."*

Current Cultural Changes in Contemporary World

In an article of his, Paul J. Bahanan writes:

> *"Ever since the mid-1800s, cultural changes accelerated at a higher rate, which was due to vast technological and industrial advances; cultural exchange has also sped up. Inventions like airplanes, cinema, radio, television, and so forth, make it possible for customs, traditions or cultures all around the world to be in constant touch. Anywhere you are, you can enjoy American jazz, English football or Japanese kimonos at the same time.*
>
> *Apparently, the expansion of cultural exchange is preparing the grounds for a global culture, and the differences among various peoples seems to be fading away. Some fear that this trend will cause man to be deprived of his long-established traditions. Others believe that the development of global cultures would lead to more variety, and enrich cultures all around the world."2*

There are a few points to consider here:

First: Science and technology have been separated from culture; this is quite considerable, since they

---

1- Gibran Khalil Gibran, *Al-mavakeb*.
2- *The World Book Encyclopedia*, Paul J. Bahanan.

naturally provide a purely scientific viewpoint, and establish a profit-orientated basis. The meritorious aspects of science and technology have unfortunately been contaminated by profiteering trends.

Second: Advances in culture development and exchange devices are highly crucial and unprecedented. If the cultural relationships and exchanges are not carefully calculated, social problems are very likely, for what is nowadays induced into people's minds as culture is not always originated from purely human emotions. If a general law – like the Human Rights – were written so that not only the study, adjustment and refining of cultures for being put into use for man's evolution, but also preventing filthy, commonplace phenomena entering other societies in the name of culture could be taken care of, original, dignified human cultures would find much more hope for survival; otherwise, they end of humanity would be inevitable.

Third: "Apparently, the expansion of cultural exchange is preparing the grounds for a global culture, and the differences among various peoples seems to be fading away."

This is not as easy as it may seem to be. By carefully studying today's cultural issues, social management trends and various systems of authority and power, we cannot come to deny the role of mighty leaders in imposing powerful society cultures. On the other hand, original, productive cultures which take account of man's highest emotions and spirits have fallen way behind technology and its characteristics nowadays. Let us return to Professor Bahanan's article, where he clearly elaborates on this fact:

"Some sociologists believe most social problems are due to the fact that some cultural elements progress more slowly than others. Most retardations in the history of the United States have been in non-physical aspects, e.g. thoughts and traditions. Science and technology advance at such

great speed that they leave non-physical cultural issues way behind."

How Cultural Aspects Can Be Transferred from One Society to Another

1.   The almighty God has provided the truth–seeking with the facts about the universe, and – due to His divine, extreme kindness, concretely confirmed in Islamic references – leaves no positively aimed efforts without fruitful result. The Koran has on several occasions emphasized on the necessity of fruitful outcomes due to efforts:

"No soul laden bears the load of another, and a man shall have to his account only as he has labored."[1]

"And who so does an atom's weight of good shall see it, and who so does an atom's weight of evil shall see it." [2]

Thus, every human being is potentially ready to receive realities by means of efforts; according to this divine-human principle, man's success in discovering truths depends on his amount of effort. This divine-human principle provides all peoples and nations with useful cultural elements, as is verified in this *hadith* by the Holy Prophet (P.B.U.H.)

"Seek knowledge, even if it may mean going all the way to China."

It was due to this belief that Muslims made great efforts ever since the rise of Islam towards acquiring the perfect cultural elements of other nations, and not only did they discover plenty of cultural and ideological realities about other cultures during the 3rd an 4th centuries (Hijra), but also fertilized them and got quite significant results with highly elevated their findings.

Thus, Islam not only never prevents adopting positive foreign cultural elements – the most apparent example to name of is science, a means of achieving the truth – but even strongly recommends it. Islam, therefore, accepts any cultural elements that can effectively discover or adopt true facts.

1- The Star (53): 39, 40.
2- The Earthquake (99): 7, 8.

It is of great importance that anthropologists distinguish real scientific issues – which are proved through concrete scientific evidence – from potentially right or wrong theories and deductions; in other words, although such theories aim to account for certain phenomena, they have not yet been definitely approved of. Studying them in anthropological fields as the mere theories or deductions they are, is quite appropriate. It would be highly useful to bring them into a society seeking development and perfection, in order to expand the humanities.

2. The current Western knowledge of the nature of man has led to a vast amount of anthropological explanations, concepts and issues so popular that they have become the source of many interpretations about various human aspects, e.g. "strong tendencies towards essential pleasures and enjoyment," which following Freud's approval, began to look like a matter of scientific significance. Apart from a very few number of wise, truth-seeking ones, most people in the West account for human issues on the basis of the highly popular hedonistic viewpoints. It is the unquestionable duty of a developing, perfectionist society to carefully seek reasons for all human aspects, and to take into serious consideration the fact whether man is naturally hedonistically orientated or not, and if he is, are the pleasures concerned with only natural, purely physical ones? Should spiritual, mental pleasures not be included? Is a society where no pleasures are based on the pains and inconveniences of others possible? In fact, such people have – using mental, social, regional and political factors – put so much emphasis on a human aspect that does not even innately exist in him that it now seems to be an essential part of human nature in the eyes of the simple-minded. Thus the establishment of Western culture nowadays is not comprehendible without taking hedonistic principles into consideration.[1]

1- For further elaboration on this point, we must mention a highly dramatic change that has occurred nowadays, and the results it has brought about:
When the West broke down all walls confining freedom and its glorious values, liberty – a vital phenomenon which is the best path to perfect virtues – turned into an undisciplined beloved which became so popular that it had the last two centuries named after it (actually, of course, named after immorality). It had

3. Some certain cultural elements originate from ethical and regional features exclusive to some nations or peoples, and thus lack a universally human quality – like taboo behaviors of tribal customs and particular interpretations of minor aspects of life. According to Islam's definition of culture (as an objective, creative culture), such elements are not only definitely unusable in anthropological issues, but even cannot be considered as ideal cultural phenomena.

4. There are other cultural elements that are compatible with intelligible human ideals. For instance, by studying religious cultures in various nations, we find that some cultural elements maybe considered unimportant in others – or maybe even illogical. A logical reasoning brings us to the conclusion that all of them originate from an extremely intelligible human ideal which has been degraded through time to a worthless phenomenon due to regional points of view and mental

---

better be called the century of "self-strangeness." Is this not a cause-and-effect outcome? Indeed, for unlimited freedom first victimizes human character. It became so sacredly worshipped that even philosophers and humanity scholars glorified undisciplined freedom to the very highest aim of life. Books like *About Freedom* by John Stuart Mill are examples of such infatuation.

Due to a small mistake between the end and the means, anyone – even the least educated – spurred by internal desires or limited knowledge, took the advantage of the necessity of freedom of speech, and expressed such exclusive, definite opinions as if they were the sole creator of man, and possessed every knowledge or experience in creation! The opinions were as greatly numerous as their so-called scholars. They were only whimsical brainwaves of philosophy and anthropology majors. On the other hand, they never thought about who should accept their ideas. Is everyone intelligent enough like Avicenna, Razi, Abu-rehyah Biruni, Mowlavi, Bacon, Descarte, Kant or Hegel to be able to correctly evaluate such opinions? Or are most of them ⇨ simple people who are prone to drown in the swamp of wrong ideas. Still, contradicting theories poured in the field of anthropology and human knowledge, which made all existing ideas doubted, and people lost most of their interest in such researches.

Some conscientious scholars could have suggested that in order to save man from such anthropological vertigo, all theories must first be analyzed alongside other fields and issues, and discussed with sincerely serious anthropologists in order to achieve a final, combined fact; when the theory showed reality, it can be publicly presented.

Even if someone in the West has come up with this suggestion – which we have not heard anything about yet – it has unfortunately been overruled.

All in all, having a society able to move towards the truth in complete independence is crucially necessary.

manipulations. We face such phenomena in various forms of worship for God. The Koran has also pointed it out.[1]

One of the commonest of human ideals that is degraded to lowly phenomena is justice – which, in its general form, is universally approved of. Since law has existed throughout the history of man, there is no exception to the fact that justice is accepted by everyone; when law exists among fellow men, every aspect of their life either obeys the law or defies it. (Let us suppose the latter is the case.) If they obey the law, justice exists; if not, there will be cruelty and deviation. However, we know that justice, in the hands of the selfish, power-greedy and ignorant people, is degraded down to a cruelly unjust phenomenon. When such cultural adjustments are transferred to anthropological domains, they will bring about nothing but obsessing people.

How Can Man – Who Accepts Culture and Cultural Activities Due to His Perfection-seeking Virtues – Openly Accept Destructive, Corrupt Cultures?

Let us first mention again that the reason why man accepts culture is his intense tendency for perfection, which is undoubtedly mighty; individual and social advances in various fields such as science and technology clearly prove it.

Now we must see why perfection-seeking human accepts destructive, corrupt factors so easily.

The most important reason for corruption is the vacuum-like gap of the realities of evolutionary culture among the society. In such an abyss, man's innate desire for perfection either will fade away, or may remain. If the former is true, lust and animal desire will dominate man's internal existence, and make any kind of corruption seem like enjoyment or even a necessity, and become the highest aim of his life. In such cases, all fundamentals like religion, ethics, law, economics, and

---

1- Lokman (31): 25: "If they are asked, 'Who created the heavens and the earth? They will say, 'God'."

politics will be manipulated by corruption, and lead the society for eventual demise.[1]

In the second case, if the innate desire for perfection still exists deep inside man, it can again be activated provided the necessary conditions, and attain original, positive cultural elements once more. If society leaders can safeguard it against corruption in fields like religion, politics, law, morality and education, and provide the grounds for its activation, the gap will obviously be filled with original, evolutionary culture. In any case, therefore, the leaders of the societies should protect their people against destruction.

The third case, which is the most dangerous form of anti-cultural invasion, is when the perfection-seeking eagerness is dominated by the "animal-like natural self." Thus, man turns into the most dangerous being, who would willingly destroy everything for just a moment of his own enjoyment.

Generally, the desire for perfection may be activated in positive or negative poles:

The *positive pole* pertains to the proper, worthy activities all Prophets, Imams (S.A.W.) and other leaders of evolutionary human movements have done in order to keep humanity from poverty or infidelity. For instance:

1.   How does the Holy Prophet Abraham (P.B.U.H.) use this force? He stands firmly against all of his friends and the people of his time in order to make faith in the only God, honesty, sincerity and other moral virtues a reality. The desire for perfection makes him carry out the task sacrificing his own child. It would be impossible to perform such a bitter task without the endless desire for perfection. With all the force Abraham had, even if he had lived for centuries, he would have done the same time and time again.

2.   The Holy Prophet Moses (P.B.U.H.) faces the atrocities of the Pharaoh for many long years, and never suffers the least

---

1- The history of Spain on many occasions states that despite Islam – the highest of divine religions – various disruptive factors deviated people from Islamic realities and emptied them from any religion, logic or conscience. If social leaders around the world do not take action against corruptive factors in the name of "culture", their people also will definitely undergo what happened in Spain.

pain. He could have kept on his resistance for years and years without any wavering or fatigue.

   3.   The history of the efforts and pains of the Holy Prophet Jesus (P.B.U.H.) needs no further explanation.

   4.   The Holy Prophet of Islam, Mohammad (P.B.U.H.) said,
   "No other prophet went through as much pain and trouble as I did."

However, he accepted the pain and trouble so eagerly as if he actually enjoyed it. Imam Ali (S.A.W.) also showed gloriously profound efforts through both pure worship and sincere services for people in order to enhance their prosperity.[1]

The *negative pole* desires unlimited "self"-power; indeed, degradation into lowly values knows no bounds.

As Neron once said: "If only all of mankind had only one head, I could cut it off with one stroke!"

Ghengis Khan be slaved many societies of his time, and still could not get enough.

Tamerlane made pillars out of the heads he cut, obsessed by the advance of his unlimited power. Those who live only for their lusts and desires consider people as their highest aim in

---

1- Michail Naima, the renowned contemporary Christian scholar thus describes Imam Ali (A.S.) in his preface to George Gordag's *Ali (A.S.), the Sound of Justice*: "The lives of great human beings overflows with experiences, lessons, faith and hope. They are high peaks that we are eagerly attracted to. As shining minarets, they light up the darkness along our way. They always remove any doubts about life, its aims and prosperity in us. Without such outstanding figures, despair would drown us; we would have raised the white flags in surrender ages ago: "O death! We are your prisoners. O death! We are your slaves. Annihilate us anyway you wish." But we never lost hope, and never will. Thus, we will triumph, as the triumphant predecessors confirm it. One of them is Abu-talib's son. Such glorious figures are always beside us (in other words, we live with them) although distantly in time and space. However, neither have time gaps made us unable to hear them, nor has spatial distance made them slip from our minds."

The book mentioned above is the best proof to what we have stated. It includes the life story of one of the greatest human beings ever born to the Arab world, although he was never deservingly used. Islam did activate his capabilities, but he did not belong to Islam alone; if he did, how could his great spirit enflame the heart of a Christian writer in Lebanon in 1956, making him carefully study the Imam's life, and create a ballad-like biography of him?

Imam Ali's (A.S.) heroism was not confined to wars. He was also a champion of chastity, intelligence and indescribable beauty, deep humanity, flaming faith, grace and generosity, helping the poor, modesty and worshipping God.

life, even if it may lead to the end of all of mankind. They not only consider their philosophy as the best for their own society, but also regard all of history as a mirror to interpret it by.

Thus, both positive and negative poles of "self"-enhancement lead to an immortal panacea; as Mowlavi states:

> *The damned wretch is an elixir which transmutes into poison and snakes; (his elixir is) contrary to the elixir of the God-fearing man* (Rumi, Masnavi, Book Two: 155).

Deculturalization Instead of Cultural Generalization

Unfortunately, culture is falling apart instead of enhancing its common cultural elements during the late 20th century; the turning point here are industrial societies, and only the power greedy, selfish authoritarians know what will eventually happen. If the curve of culture continues to fall into a nosedive, we would be quite lucky if it just degrades us back to our cave days. The "new" culture it advertises deploys every scientific or artistic effort in order to establish animal instincts, and take people far away from highly moral virtues.

We had better call it the "anti-culture", or "deculturalization" of human societies. It tends to deliver the final blow to humanity: first demolish human realities and fundamental values, destroy the sacred foundation called "family", and eventually call the whole earth a useless part of the solar system, and ruin it.

May God save mankind once again from those who destroy human values and deculturalize humanity, and grant us deliverance by enhancing our logic, reason and conscience.[1]

1- It is not from a solely metaphysical point of view that we pray that God may save all of mankind from the selfish and powerful. Consider the following story, which I have cited in several of my works due to its high significance. In 1949, Einstein thus described a discussion he had with a high American official: "Recently, I was speaking to one of America's more intellectual, good-willing figures. I warned him about the new war that was threatening mankind, and that it could destroy the whole of humanity, and only super-national organizations could stop it. But he amazingly replied, 'Why do you so strongly disagree with the end of mankind?!' Einstein adds, "Such a straightforward, abrupt answer implies the intense, internal suffering the world today has led to.

A global culture depends directly on the globalization of the four fundamental realities:

1. global human economy,
2. global human power,
3. global human rights, and
4. global human politics.

Let us elaborate further by addressing:

Such answer can only come from somebody who has put much effort into balancing his character, but has failed, and even lost hope. It depicts the painful, innate isolation all humans are suffering from." See Philip Frank, *The Life of Einstein*.

Global Culture

1. The idea of achieving a global culture for people of all nations and societies is a great human ideal that anyone aware of man's nature, physical and spiritual needs and commonalities would warmly approve of. The strongest reason for the universal agreement on this matter is the generality of the humanities and literary culture that covers all nations and peoples, and is the same for Asians, Africans or Europeans.

2. By "global culture" we do not refer to all elements and phenomena, for any society innately has certain characteristics in regard to religion, the universe and fellow men that are exclusive to its own historical, geographical and social factors.

What we mean by global culture are the general realities of culture, such as fundamental moral virtues (love for fellowmen, sacrificing for human ideals), accepting a worthy, meritorious life for mankind, accepting intelligible (responsible) freedom for all, and accepting to try hard to advance man's highest goals.

If the four above-mentioned fundamentals (global human economy, global human power, global human rights, and global human politics) are logically established, global culture is obviously achievable. We realize that all divine religions – originating from Abraham's – based upon man's pure, innate virtues (especially Islam, which covers all of their basics) would warmly accept such a culture. If all human societies do not possess the four fundamentals, this culture will never be able to exist.

The reason why is quite clear. Considering the definition for culture (the proper, worthy or meritorious qualities for man's physical or spiritual life phenomena or activities based on logic and emotions originating from *intelligible life*), no society can enjoy a dynamic, objective evolutionary culture by means of an imperfect economy, lack of establishment for people's physical or spiritual enhancement or a legal system truly addressing social requirements and realities, for throughout the history of politics and power, when Machiavellians have taken control, humanity and its values have unfortunately been victimized. If powerful politicians are the end and people are the means" is the key motto to achieve political control, there will be no room for values like religion, morals, law, socioeconomics, politics or even culture – the ideas of Ghengis Khans and Nerons proves this.

Appendix*

Let us first consider the ideas of several Western scholars on the history of science in Islamic societies:

John Bernal has written:

"Islam has been the religion of science and knowledge from the very beginning. Furthermore, unlike the Roman Empire, Islamic cities did not isolate themselves from the rest of the East. Islam was where Asian and European sciences met. Thus, inventions were made that were totally unknown -or even unachievable- to Greek or Roman technology, such as steel products, silk paper and enameled chinaware. Such inventions also led to other advances, bringing about more activity in the West, and eventually the 17th and 18th industrial revolutions." [1]

Isaac Asimov explains:

"In the seventh century, the Arabs conquered Damascus, and then Egypt, thus inheriting a vast treasure of Greek knowledge and science.

This historical point is highly significant, for if Muslims hadn't become so powerful and sophisticated, the whole civilized world might have become a battlefield for barbarian tribes.

During the thousand years of the Byzantine Empire, science and technology were completely forsaken among the intense struggles and battles for power. Calinicus was the only glitter of science and wisdom in that era. Western Europe was in a deep sleep of ignorance and darkness. The Muslims were the only guardians of science. They not only saved Greek science and philosophy by translating them, but also enriched science with their amazing works of research and excellent books. Alchemy was of particular interest to them." [2]

Sigrid Hunke agrees:

---

* This appendix has been compiled from Allameh Jafari's *Interpretation of the Nahj-ol-balagheh*, Vols. 19 and 22.

1- John Bernal, *Science in History*.

2- Isaac Asimov, *The Encyclopedia of Science and Industry*.

"We have inherited science and technology not only from Rome and Greece, but also from the world of Islamic thought. The West undoubtedly owes Islam a great deal."

Philip Hatta adds:

"No civilization achieved as much scientific progress during the medieval era as the Muslims did."

John Bernal writes:

"The Muslims were culturally independent, and received a warm welcome having conquered the Mediterranean areas… In fact, it would have been more logical to consider the history of science confined to the period between the seventh (1st century Hijra) and fourteenth centuries…The basic topics (of Islamic culture) are interestingly not only worldly, but also scientific. This is why Christian universities followed Islamic methods… It was the Muslims who taught the Europeans how to make and use paper in the 12th century." [1]

We must remember that since the final end of Islam is achieving a *intelligible life,* posing the question whether Islam considers science necessary or not, is like asking whether Islam considers intelligible life a necessity or not, for science – discovering reality – is a part of the context of intelligible life. If we study almost 700 Koranic verses and hundreds of *hadith* cited in reliable Islamic reference books, we will find that Islam believes that living without a knowledge of the realities of man and the universe is not living at all, and realize how ridiculous it is to question the value of science in Islam. In order to study the influence of these references on Muslims, it is best to refer to the great number of Muslim scientists and scholars throughout history.

1- John Bernal, *Science in History.*

Bertrand Russell admits:

> "The Muslims had a more experimental approach in their scientific research – particularly in chemistry – than the Greek, They endeavored to turn cheap metals into gold, discover the secrets of alchemy and reach the elixir of life, because they had a deep respect for chemistry.
>
> During all the years of ignorant and darkness, it was the Muslims who actually advanced civilization, and any knowledge gained by late medieval scholars, like Roger Bacon, was based on Islamic science." [1]

Aldo Mili writes:

> "Arabic knowledge, which provided the basis for the new European civilization, lost its worldwide acclaim in the 13th century.

Alfred North Whitehead adds:

> "The Byzantine and the Muslims were civilizations themselves, so their cultures retained their innate forces, reinforced by physical and spiritual adventures. They traded with the Far East and widened their territory in the West, made laws, created new forms of art, took and analytical approach to theology, revolutionized mathematics and enriched medicine." [2]

George Sarton believes:

> "Perhaps the most significant – but still the least visible – scientific development during the medieval era, was the establishment of empirical thought. The Muslims made possible the progress of this way of thinking up to the 12th century...Even a brief description of how Islam has developed science would exceed the capacity of this book. They did far more than just translating Greek scientific references. They not only passed science on to the next generations, but also provided their own innovations.
>
> Creating a new universal excellent scientific civilization in less than two centuries is quite an achievement, andwe cannot praise it enough." [3]

1- John Bernal, *Science in History.*
2- Alfred North Whitehead, *The Story of Thoughts.*
3- George Sarton, *The Story of Science.*

In Allah's Sun Shines on the West, **Sigrid Hunke adds:**
"Using their scientific research and experience, the Muslims changed the raw material they got from the Greek into a new face of science. In fact, it was the Muslims who established the role of experience in scientific endeavor... Not only did the Arabs save the Greek civilization from fading away, but also introduced empirical scientific methods in chemistry, natural sciences, arithmetic, algebra, zoology, trigonometry and social sciences. Furthermore, many of their inventions and discoveries in various fields of science were stolen or pertained to others."
Gustav Le Bon, the French researcher, believes:
"Up to the 15th century, no quotation was credited unless it had been quoted by the (Muslim) Arabs. George Bacon, Leonardo da Vinci, Arnold, Raymond Loli, Villano, St. Thomas, Great Albert and Alfons the Tenth were either trained in Islamic schools or wrote about them. Renagne, the French philosopher believes that the Great Albert learned all he knew from Avicenna, and St. Thomas' philosophy originates from Ibn Rushd. For 500 to 600 years books written by Muslims dominated European textbooks."[1]
Let us return to John Bernal, who has divided great scientific endeavors into three periods:
"There have been three great periods of scientific endeavors: 9th -century Islam, 11th-century Spain and 13th-century France."

Thus, can we still claim that Muslims imitated others' science?

Their empirical method was not incidental; it is derived from Islamic reference books. Imam Ali (A.S.) has frequently emphasized the necessity of science. Here are a few of his *hadith* on this matter:

1- *Experience leads to new science.* [2]
2- *There are two types of wisdom: natural and experience-based. Both are quite advantageous.* [3]
3- *The value of man's ideas depends on his experience.* [4]

1- Gustave Le Bon, *The Islamic and Arab Civilization.*
2- Hassan ibn Ali ibn Shu'ba, *Tohaf-ol-oghoul.*
3- Allameh Majlesi, *Behar-ol-anvar.*
4- Abdul-vahed Amedi, *Ghorar-ol-hekam va Dorar-ol-kalem.*

4- *Accurate calculation leads to success and it is experience can cause accurate calculation.*

5- *Wisdom lies in keeping and using one's experience.* [1]

6- *Cruel is the one who deprives himself of the treasure of wisdom and experience he has.* [2]

Let us now take a look at some of the libraries built by Muslims:

1.   *The library of the observatory at Maragheh, built by Khajeh Nasir-il-din Tousi, containing 400,000 books.*

2.   *The library of Najaf in the 10th century (about the time Sheikh Tousi lived) contained 40,000 books.*

3.   *During the reign of the Baghdad qalifs, one library had 100,000 books.*

4.   *Azizi, the qalif of Cairo, had a library containing 1,600,000 books, 6500 volumes of which were on mathematics and 18000 others on philosophy. His son, as his successor, did a great deal to develop the library, and built 18 study halls near it.*

In addition, governers and viziers throughout history have played a significant role in gathering books and constructing libraries that paved the path toward scientific advance. Mahlabi left after his death a library of 170,000 books. His young colleague, Saheb-ibn-Ibad, had collected 206000 books, and one of Saheb's judges had collected over a hundred thousand books. These figures are, nevertheless, approximate.Many librarians were busy working in Cairo, where only two of the libraries had 2,200,000 books. In 891, there were a hundred libraries in Baghdad." 3

1-*Nahj-ol-balagheh*, Letter No. 31 (Imam Ali's letter to Imam Hassan).
2- Ibid., Letter No. 78.
3- Sigrid Hunke, *Allah's Sonne Uber den Abendland (Allah's Sun Shines Upon the West)*

Allameh Muhammad Taghi Jafari

(1923-1998)

About the Author

Muhammad Taghi Ja'fari (born 1923, Tabriz, Iran, and died 1998) was a contemporary sage and an expert in philosophy and Islamic knowledge. Ja'fari was familiar with Western culture and also with the needs of modern human being and the contemporary culture. He was indeed an original and innovative thinker.

One of the most important innovations of this honorable master was that he, like Allameh Tabatabaei and Sayyed Muhammad Bagher Sadr, used the methodology of comparative studies for introducing Islamic knowledge to a generation who was thirsty for truth. Indeed, Ja'fari has left us a collection of invaluable works on Islamic teachings, philosophy of arts, aesthetics, literature, mysticism, the study of the *Nahjulbalaghah*, psychology, human rights and pedagogy.

In addition to being an expert in philosophy, in Islamic mysticism and in *Fiqh* (jurisprudence), Ja'fari was familiar with the works and the ideas of classical Western philosophers such as Socrates, Plato, and Aristotle. He was also versed in the works of modern philosophers including Descartes, Leibniz, Hume, Kant, Hegel, and contemporary philosophers such as Balzac, Dostoevsky, Tolstoy, Hugo, and modern-day physicists including Max Planck, and Einstein.

Ja'fari's epistemic geometry comprises of the knowledge of the mind, the revelation and the heart, tradition and modernity, physics and metaphysics, law and aesthetics. While the first three sources were the main pillars of his thinking, the expressions of his thoughts were nonetheless the result of dialogues made on the different bases of this epistemic geometry, which – due to their up-to-date nature – made his works novel and attentive to the debates on the difficulties of the "modern human" and the "modern life".

Ja'fari's 15-volume *Rumi: the Man and His Ideas, an Interpretation, Criticism and Analysis of Rumi's Masnavi* and his 27-volume *Translation and Interpretation of the Nahjulbalaghah* have a distinct place in his body of work. In terms of the clergies' principles, attending to Rumi's *Masnavi* was a heresy, or disliked to say the least. Moreover, writing commentaries on the *Nahjulbalaghah* was considered as a virtue, not a science. Scholarship was, and still is seen as footnoting on important books on *fiqh* (jurisprudence). It was in such an environment that the honorable master instilled *Masnavi* back in the minds of students and academicians. By comparing Rumi's sublime and amorous assertions with those of French and Russian thinkers and scholars, with whom Iranian intellectuals are more familiar, he once again took Rumi's *Masnavi* back into Iranian homes, in which households were more acquainted with Western culture. Afterwards, by writing an exegesis on the *Nahjulbalaghah*, entitled "A Manifesto on Wisdom, Mysticism and Politics," he familiarized the younger generation with an Islam devoid of superstition, factionalism and backwardness, an Islam based on the mind, revelation, justice and love. We can consider Ja'fari as the vanguard in writing commentaries on Rumi's *Masnavi* and the *Nahjulbalaghah* in the contemporary era, to whom all the later commentators are indebted.

According to Allameh Ja'fari, love and the mind are the two wings that make humans fly towards the absolute truth. The mind and revelation, science and religion, the mind and *shari'a* (Islamic law) are all compatible and do not contradict one another. Of course, the mind is the solid pillar of knowing (episteme). In his thoughts on the political principles of Islam, he saw justice, compassion, mercy, tolerance, serving the people, and reliance on consultation (*Shura*) and also on people's decisions as the basis of Islamic governance.

In terms of personal character and ethical manner, despite his high stature, Ja'fari was humble and modest. Unlike some learned scholars, he did not consider himself as someone who knew everything; there was no trace of arrogance and contemptuousness in him. Throughout his productive life, he preferred the trappings of science by devoting himself wholeheartedly to the cultivation of intellectual life.

He passed away on 15 November, 1998 suffering from a cancer disease in London. He was buried in Dar-Al-Zohd, by Imam Reza's Holy Shrine in Mashhad.

The Allameh Jafari Institute

www.ingramcontent.com/pod-product-compliance
Lightning Source LLC
Chambersburg PA
CBHW051627120626
46551CB00014B/1965